G.FUMAGALLI

LOVERS

in Art

LOVERS
in Art

MEREDITH JOHNSON

PORTLAND HOUSE
New York

Contents

This 1991 edition was published by Portland House, a division of dilithium Press, Ltd., distributed by Outlet Book Company, Inc, a Random House Company, 225 Park Avenue South, New York, New York 10003

8 7 6 5 4 3 2 1
ISBN 0-517-03745-9
Printed and bound in Hong Kong
Lovers in Art was prepared and produced by Moore & Moore Publishing, 11 W. 19th Street, New York, New York 10011

AN M&M BOOK
Project Director & Editor Gary Fishgall
Senior Editorial Assistant Shirley Vierheller; *Editorial Assistants* Maxine Dormer, Ben D'Amprisi, Jr; *Photo Research* Maxine Dormer, Jana Marcus, Janice Ostan.
Designer Binns & Lubin
Separations and Printing Regent Publishing Services Ltd.

Measurements of the paintings are in inches, height before width.

PAGE 2 TER BORCH, *Woman Playing the Theorbo* (detail)

PHOTO CREDITS
Art Institute of Chicago 71, 139; Artothek, Munich 82, 113; Ashmolean Museum 78; Bridgeman/SuperStock, Inc. 16, 17, 24-25, 32, 36-37, 70, 75, 76-77, 79, 89, 110, 117, 122-123, 129, 142-143, 145, 168-169; Cliché Musées d'Angers 83; Department of Near Eastern and Classical Antiquities, The National Museum, Denmark 111; Giraudon/Art Resource 158-159; Islamisches Museum der Staatliche Museen zu Berlin 50; Landesmuseum, Mainz 146-147; Mauritshuis, The Hague 138; The Metropolitan Museum of Art 29, 38, 41, 51, 54, 68, 69, 99, 130-131, 152-153, 157, 163; Minneapolis Institute of Arts 39, 46-47; Musée National D'Art Moderne, Centre National d'Art et de Culture Georges Pompidou, Photo Philippe Migeat 108; Museo del Prado, Madrid 86-87, 162; Museum of Fine Arts, Boston 112; The Museums at Stony Brook, Stony Brook, New York 144; National Gallery of Art, Washington, D.C. 55, 67, 148; The National Gallery, London 40, 80-81, 85, 106, 119, 126-127, 150-151; Norton Gallery of Art, West Palm Beach, Florida 132-133; Philadelphia Museum of Art 66; Photothèque des Musées de la Ville de Paris; 27; Riccar Art Museum, Tokyo 13; Rijksmuseum, Amsterdam 96; Rose Art Museum, Brandeis University 147; The Royal Collection, Copyright Reserved to Her Majesty Queen Elizabeth II 128; San Diego Museum of Art 21; Scala/Art Resource 140-141; Sheldon Memorial Art Gallery, University of Nebraska-Lincoln 124-125; Smith College Museum of Art 98; S.P.A.D.E.M./Réunion des Musées Nationaux 14-15, 30-31, 33, 74; Staatliche Museen Preussischer Kulturbesitz Nationalgalerie, Berlin 48-49/Antikenmuseum 53; Staatliche Kunstsammlungen, Dresden 20; SuperStock, Inc. 23, 26, 44-45, 52, 58, 59, 90, 91, 97, 102, 104-105, 114-115, 116, 123, 166; Daniel J. Terra Collection, Terra Museum of American Art, Chicago 109; Toledo Museum of Art 118; Trustees of Sir John Soane's Museum 88; Victoria & Albert Museum 154-155.

Introduction

"Any time that is not spent on love is wasted," wrote the Renaissance poet Torquato Tasso, and the countless couples represented in the world's vast treasury of art bear witness to the importance of love in the human imagination. Flirtatious, seductive, devoted, faithful, generous, cruel or disillusioned, lovers appear throughout history in the art of virtually all cultures, offering a complete catalogue of human behavior for our contemplation and enjoyment. No less varied are the styles and sensibilities of the artists who have described lovers in paintings, sculptures, drawings, and prints. In their works, we encounter humor, compassion, and poetry.

Chosen from a limitless wealth of possibilities, the images in this book explore four main aspects of romantic love: courtship, passion, marriage, and separation or loss. A postscript deals with the imaginary garden of love, a vision of a timeless, pastoral paradise for lovers that has haunted the human imagination since antiquity.

Courtship passes unrecorded in the art of some cultures, while in others, its many rituals and activities are copiously illustrated. Occasionally, it has risen to become one of the primary subjects of the artist, as was the case with the medieval notion of courtly love. For several centuries, the selfless devotion pledged by a knight to his lady found visual expression in tapestries, manuscript illuminations, and a host of decorative objects. Like all powerful ideas, the concept of unselfish courtly devotion outlived its creators. Echoes of the notion can be found in Nicholas Hilliard's Renaissance miniature of an elegant courtier loyally wearing the colors of his queen, or in Edouard Manet's small painting of violets and a fan, presented as a courtly tribute to his friend, the painter Berthe Morisot.

Love letters, flowers, lingering looks, and moonlit walks all make their appearance in these pages, reminding the viewer of the enormous variety of styles and attitudes with which artists of differing times and places have approached similar subjects. A single theme such as the relation between musical harmony and love may call forth the delicate eroticism of *Two Lovers Playing a Samisen* by the 18th-century Japanese artist Suzuki Harunobu, or the lyrical melancholy of *Mezzetin*, by the 18th-century French artist Antoine Watteau.

Not surprisingly, the most frequent artistic representation of courting couples appears in cultures most interested in representing the daily activities of their own lives, such as 17th-century Holland, or in cultures seized by a romantic idea of flirtation and courtship, such as rococo France. A similar ebb and flow occurs in the frequency with which passionate love finds expression in the visual arts. The pleasures of physical love may be represented with a matter-of-fact acceptance reflecting the survival of ancient fertility imagery, as is sometimes the case with Greek or Roman art, or they may be presented as the latest fashion in urban decadence, as in William Hogarth's *The Orgy* and Edouard Manet's *Nana*. Among the most prolific and dedicated chroniclers of erotic experience were the *ukiyo-e* printmakers of 18th- and 19th-century Japan. Their images of the "floating world" included illustrated guides to the famous courtesans of Tokyo and collections of erotic prints, each preceded by a more decorous frontispiece.

If courtship and passion are variable themes in art, the solidarity of marriage is one of the most constant. The enduring affection conveyed by the sculpture of the Egyptian King Mycerinus and his queen speaks to us clearly across the centuries, as does the tenderness expressed by the anonymous Etruscan couple represented on a sarcophagus from Cerveteri. Married couples represented in art range from the appealing youthfulness of Mary Stuart and Prince William of Orange, whose wedding portrait was painted by Sir Anthony Van Dyck, to the unspoken intimacy of the elderly couple movingly portrayed by their son, the American artist Raphael Soyer. Jan van Eyck's great painting, *The Marriage of Giovanni Arnolfini* at once serves as an extraordinarily vivid eyewitness account of a particular wedding ceremony and as a symbolic testimony to the sanctity of marriage itself.

The inevitability of parting and loss also finds varied expression in the visual arts. The silent tension that can occur between couples is forcefully presented in Edgar Degas' *Interior* and in Henri Matisse's *Conversation*, whereas Jan Steen's *The Lovesick Maiden* takes a more humorous and satirical look at the pain of a jilted lover. Grief over the death of a beloved may be represented with the dramatic and classicizing rhetoric of Frederic Leighton's *Lacrymae*, or it may be implicitly present in the direct and understated naturalism of Claude Monet's painting of his wife on her deathbed.

The limitations imposed on love by mortality and the vicissitudes of life have given rise to an enduring dream of a paradisical landscape in which love is openly expressed and unencumbered by necessity or care. This vision of a garden of love is represented by works as diverse as Giorgione's *Concert Champêtre*, which created a lasting and influential pictorial representation of this ideal, and its 20th-century descendant, Wassily Kandinsky's abstract painting *Improvisation Number 27: The Garden of Love*.

A single book can do no more than show a miniscule sample of the avalanche of works devoted to lovers and couples. Rather than attempt to incorporate a representative survey of world art, this volume presents a greater number of works from cultures particularly rich in romantic or erotic images, such as rococo France and Edo-era Japan.

The styles of the artists whose work is illustrated in these pages is no less varied than their subjects, and the reader will encounter a broad spectrum of approaches to art, from the monumental serenity of Egyptian sculpture, to the painterly brilliance of Titian, and the incisive draftsmanship of Moronobu. Equally diverse are the artists' attitudes towards their subjects, which range from the satirical humor of Jan Steen and William Hogarth to the deep compassion of Rembrandt. Each of these works also conveys something of the character of the artist who created it, whether it is the subtle wit of Paul Klee or the poetic melancholy of Antoine Watteau.

In following the progress of love from the first moments of youthful courtship to the unconscious unity of old married couples, this book echoes one of the most persistent themes in poetry and art: the relationship between love and time. "Gather ye rosebuds while ye may," wrote the British poet Robert Herrick. The notion of love offered as a challenge to time and to human mortality is implicit in much of the art and in the introductory poems included in this book.

The author wishes to express gratitude and appreciation to the many friends and colleagues who were unfailingly generous with help and encouragement. This book is dedicated to her parents, James and Beverley Day.

Courtship

Had we but world enough, and time,
This coyness, Lady, were no crime.
We would sit down and think which way
To walk and pass our long love's day.
Thou by the Indian Ganges' side
Shouldst rubies find: I by the tide
Of Humber would complain. I would
Love you ten years before the Flood,
And you should, if you please, refuse
Till the conversion of the Jews.
My vegetable love should grow
Vaster than empires, and more slow;
An hundred years should go to praise
Thine eyes and on thy forehead gaze;
Two hundred to adore each breast;
But thirty thousand to the rest;
An age at least to every part,
And the last age should show your heart;
For, Lady, you deserve this state,
Nor would I love at lower rate.

But at my back I always hear
Time's winged chariot hurrying near;
And yonder all before us lie
Deserts of vast eternity.
Thy beauty shall no more be found,
Nor, in thy marble vault, shall sound
My echoing song: then worms shall try
That long preserved virginity,
And your quaint honour turn to dust,
And into ashes all my lust:
The grave's a fine and private place,
But none, I think, do there embrace.
Now therefore, while the youthful hue
Sits on thy skin like morning dew,
And while thy willing soul transpires
At every pore with instant fires,
Now let us sport us while we may,
And now, like amorous birds of prey,
Rather at once our time devour
Than languish in his slow-chapt power.
Let us roll all our strength and all
Our sweetness up into one ball,
And tear our pleasures with rough strife
Thorough the iron gates of life:
Thus, though we cannot make our sun
Stand still, yet we will make him run.

ANDREW MARVELL
To His Coy Mistress

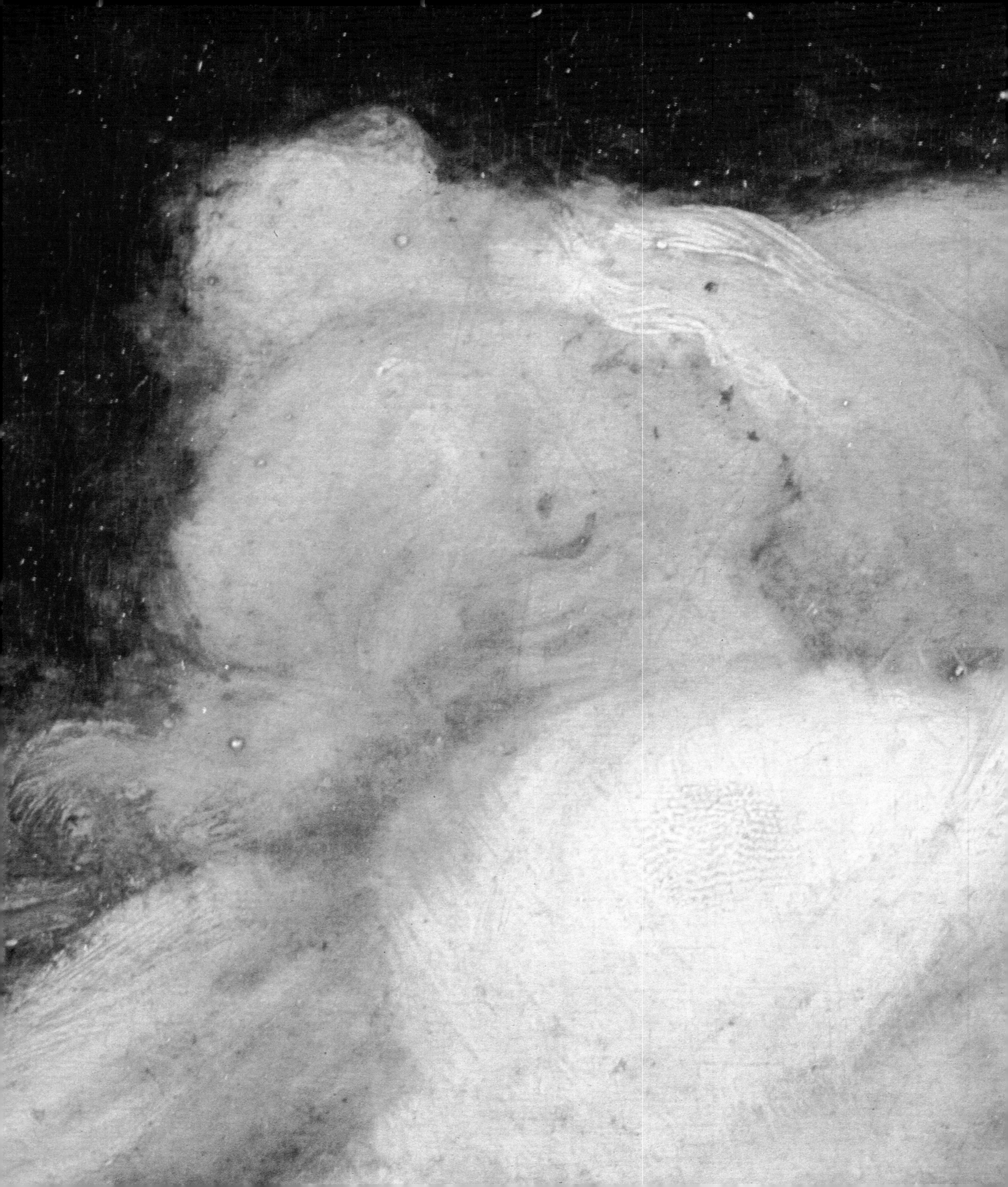

♣ *Invocation to Love*

Which comes first, a lover or the desire to love? The two young girls represented here are engaged in very private moments of communion with the idea of love. Perhaps these rituals relate to specific lovers, but they may express more generalized longings.

In *The Vow to Love*, Jean-Honoré Fragonard's young girl flings herself passionately toward a statue of a cupid with an intensity suggesting that she is seeking to further the progress of a romance in full bloom. A mysterious light falls on her flying figure and separates it from the dark woods surrounding her. The poetic force of this small oil sketch impressed French critics when it was exhibited in Paris in 1860, and one of them, Paul de Saint-Victor, wrote "It is not even a sketch, hardly a smudge. . . . A girl, or rather a cloud in the form of a woman, throws herself upon an altar plunged in darkness. Come no closer! The slightest breath would dissolve this vaporous apparition! But what soul carries away this ethereal form? It is the incarnation of a burning sigh."

In Ishikawa Toyonobu's *Girl Tying Verse to Cherry Branch*, a young woman is reaching up to tie a wistful love poem to a tree. The poem reads: "On meeting again, there will be sorrows / How fleeting are the cherry blossoms." Behind her, a curtain emblazoned with a large black crest screens her from a group of people who have come to view the cherry blossoms. A corner of the rug that they have brought with them peeks out from behind the curtain. The serpentine trunk of the cherry tree forms a harmonious counterpoint to the curves of the girl's richly patterned kimono.

Toyonobu was an early practitioner of

DETAIL
The Vow of Love
JEAN-HONORE FRAGONARD

Girl Tying Verse to Cherry Branch, late 1740s
ANJODO ISHIKAWA SHUHA TOYONOBU, Japanese, 1711–1785
Riccar Art Museum, Tokyo. Handcolored woodblock print, 19¾ x 9 in.

the Japanese woodblock prints known as *ukiyo-e*, or images of the "floating world" of everyday life. These sophisticated and colorful prints often represented courtesans, famous actors, and fashionable urban pleasures. They were enormously popular in Japan for more than 200 years and were collected eagerly by French artists when they made their first appearance in Europe in the mid-19th century. In contrast to later *ukiyo-e*, which were generally printed in color, this one was produced in black and hand colored.

The Vow to Love, c. 1780
JEAN-HONORE FRAGONARD, French, 1732–1806
Musée du Louvre, Paris. Oil on panel, 9 3/8 x 12 5/8 in.

The pensive figure in Nicholas Hilliard's miniature *A Young Man Leaning Against a Tree Among Roses* is the epitome of Elizabethan courtly elegance. Standing gracefully and a little theatrically, with his hand pressed to his heart, he has long been seen as a romantic figure or perhaps a lovesick youth. Recently he has been identified as Robert Devereaux, second earl of Essex, a member of the court of Queen Elizabeth I, and a friend of the poet Philip Sidney. He is surrounded by tiny pink blossoms of eglantine, a flower associated with Queen Elizabeth, and he wears her colors of black and white. His pose probably represents the chivalrous devotion of a courtier to his queen. A Latin inscription at the top of the miniature translates as "Praised faith gives wounds." It may refer to Devereaux's efforts to regain the queen's favor after her displeasure with his covert marriage to Philip Sidney's widow.

Dance of Mirth is an illustration from a 16th-century edition of *The Romance of the Rose*, an allegorical poem of chivalrous love written in the 13th century. The poem enjoyed tremendous popularity for several hundred years and was copied or printed in many versions. This hand-painted illustration is from the greatest of the surviving manuscripts. The book-length poem told the story of the Lover and his quest for the Rose, a symbol of romantic love. Struck with arrows by the God of Love as he contemplated the flower, the young man fell in love with it and pursued it through a series of adventures and trials.

The illustration reproduced here is from an early part of the poem, before the young man's first encounter with the Rose. Arising early on a May morning, he has entered a walled orchard, where elegant couples are singing with musicians. The young man, who can be seen on the left edge of the picture, is approached by a woman who invites him to dance. A procession of carolers winds toward the musicians, led by Sir Mirth and his companion Gladness. The winged God of Love walks behind him with Beauty, and they are followed by others, including Lady Wealth, Lady Largesse, and at the rear, Candor with her knight. These fashionable courtiers recall the opulence of the 15th-century Burgundian court, where the manuscript was commissioned. Surrounding the scene is a wide border filled with birds, flowers, and insects, rendered with great delicacy and naturalism.

A Young Man Leaning Against a Tree Among Roses, c. 1588

NICHOLAS HILLIARD, British, c. 1547–1619

Victoria and Albert Museum, London. Body color on vellum, 5 1/4 x 2 7/8 in.

Dance of Mirth from the *Roman de la Rose*

Harley Manuscript 4425, Folio 14 v.

BRUGES, c. 1490–1500

British Library, London. painted on vellum, 15 3/8 x 11 3/8 in.

FOLLOWING PAGES: DETAIL *Dance of Mirth*

Ceste gent dont
je vous parole
S'estoient pris
a la carole
Et une dame leur chantoit
Qui liesse appellee estoit
Bien sceut chanter et plaisamment
Plus que nulle et mignotement
Son bel refrain moult bien lui sist
Car de chanter merveilles fist

Elle avoit la voix clere et saine
Laquelle n'estoit pas villaine
Tres bien se savoit debriser
Ferir du pie et remoiser
Les gens la tenoient moult chiere
Pource qu'elle estoit la premiere
De belle face et planiere
Courtoise estoit et non pas fiere
De joyeusete fut marrine
Et aussi de solas fourine

♣ *Flowers*

Flowers have long been associated with love because of their beauty, freshness, and fragrance. Their short-lived fragility has served as a metaphor for the brevity of human life. Countless poems link flowers with the transience of youth and the necessity of accepting love while youth and beauty last.

In Rembrandt's *Portrait of Saskia*, the artist's wife presses one hand against her heart while in the other, she holds a tiny flower as if offering it to the viewer. Her head and hands are bathed in light, and she looks outward with a clear-eyed and appealing expression. Rembrandt portrayed Saskia twice as Flora, a goddess of spring, during the first years of their marriage. In those costume paintings, she was adorned with masses of flowers and carried a garlanded staff. In this picture, she is dressed conventionally, if elegantly, and only the single blossom recalls Rembrandt's more extravagant floral tributes to her youthful loveliness.

In Winslow Homer's *Woman with a Rose*, a young woman gazes intently at a flower that she holds against her breast. She wears a white summer dress and her face is shadowed as she bends in contemplation. Although the subject of the watercolor is clearly a romantic one, Homer's approach to it is serious and straightforward, and completely devoid of the sentimentality often found in 19th-century images of love and lovers. The sturdy young woman standing in the sunlight is rather plainly dressed by Victorian standards and appears to be without any coquettish awareness of the viewer.

Portrait of Saskia, 1641
REMBRANDT HARMENSZ. VAN RIJN, Dutch, 1606–1669
Staatlische Kunstsammlungen, Dresden. Oil on canvas, 38½ x 32⅛ in.

Woman with a Rose, c. 1879
WINSLOW HOMER, American, 1836–1910
San Diego Museum of Art. Watercolor on paper, 12 x 8 in.

♣ *The Swing*

Tossed aloft in a shaded landscape of feathery trees, a young girl kicks her tiny pink slipper toward a statue of cupid. Her admirer leans backward in rapture as her foaming petticoats lift to reveal an indiscreet length of stockinged leg. Jean-Honoré Fragonard's famous painting *The Swing* captures the lighthearted, amorous *joie de vivre* that is the hallmark of French rococo art.

Swings appeared frequently in French art of the 18th century, where they were associated with idleness, play, and flirtation. In many paintings, young women on swings were pulled by friends or admirers holding ropes. Their back and forth motions were meant to suggest flirtatious indecision or to serve as an erotic metaphor for the act of love. The specific details of the scene represented in Fragonard's *The Swing* were set forth decisively by the man who commissioned the painting, the Baron de Saint-Julien, an official in the French clergy. The baron initially offered the commission to the artist Gabriel-François Doyen in 1767, shortly after he had won a medal for a religious painting. Doyen confided to a friend, "He asked me to paint madame (pointing out to me his mistress) on a swing being pushed by a bishop. I was to place him in such a way that he could see the legs of this beautiful child, and even more. . . ." The horrified Doyen referred Saint-Julien to Fragonard.

In the hands of a lesser artist, this kind of commission might have produced a piece of heavy-handed, leering erotica, but Fragonard redeemed the subject with his tact and with his evident joy in the exuberant, natural abundance of the flower-strewn landscape. In place of the bishop, Fragonard represented an older layman pushing the swing, and he depicted an admirer too youthful to be Saint-Julien.

The Swing, c. 1767

JEAN-HONORE FRAGONARD, French, 1732–1806

Wallace Collection, London. Oil on canvas
30 x 25½ in.

manet, 1879

♣ A Chance Encounter

Edouard Manet was a keen and subtle observer of Parisian life, and he took great pleasure in recording the manners and social habits of his contemporaries. In *Chez le Père Lathuille*, he depicts an incident taking place on the garden terrace of a well-known restaurant near the northern outskirts of Paris. A young man dressed in the bohemian smock of an artist crouches beside the table of a well-dressed older woman, who has been lunching alone. The plate of fruit between her hands, the empty tables in the background, and the waiter hovering nearby with a coffeepot indicate the lateness of the hour. Holding the woman's wineglass in one hand and reaching across the back of her chair with the other arm, the young man is clearly bent on conquest as he gazes intently into her face. The woman appears to be intensely uncomfortable as she sits stiffly forward in her chair, avoiding his outstretched arm.

The theme of a young man courting an older woman met by chance in a public place is a common one in the novels of the time, and this sort of accidental but highly charged encounter between strangers was seen as typical of the modern, urban world by artists and writers of 19th-century Paris.

Manet painted this scene from models posed in his studio, yet the loosely painted background gives a sense of outdoor sunlight. Indeed, the edge of the waiter's apron seems to shimmer and dissolve in the light. From 1870 onward, Manet lightened his color palette in response to the work of his younger contemporaries, the Impressionists, who had begun to paint landscapes outdoors, in *plein-air*. In spite of his interest in their discoveries, Manet remained faithful to his lifelong fascination with the urban life of modern Paris.

Chez le Père Lathuille, 1879
EDOUARD MANET, French, 1832–1883
Musée des Beaux-Arts, Tournai. Oil on canvas, 36¼ x 44 in.

♣ A Country Dance

Pierre Auguste Renoir's painting *Dance at Bougival* is the first of three pictures of dancing couples that the artist completed in 1882 and 1883. The dancers in this picture are enjoying themselves at an outdoor cafe at Bougival, one of the many suburban pleasure resorts that had sprung up in the environs of Paris. The young man clasps his partner firmly around the waist and leans forward eagerly as she turns shyly away from him. Her skirt billows out as they turn on a dance floor littered with discarded matches and a fallen bunch of violets. Other figures are visible in the tree-shaded background. The model for the dancing man was Renoir's friend Paul Lhote, a writer, and the model for his partner was the 17-year-old Marie-Clementine Valadon, who later became well-known as the painter Suzanne Valadon.

The Lovers in the Country, Sentiments of Youth, Paris, attributed to Gustave Courbet, is a second version of a painting that the artist exhibited in 1846 as *The Waltz*. It shows Courbet dancing in the country twilight with a woman who is probably his lover, Virginie Binet. The sketchily painted sky is full of dark clouds, and the last rays of the setting sun can be seen at the left. The two half-length figures are lit strongly from above. Courbet, who was proud of his angular, "Assyrian" profile, tilts his head toward the viewer, causing deep shadows to fall across his features, while his partner's face is clearly illuminated, emphasizing the pearly, translucent texture of her skin.

Dance at Bougival, 1882–1883
PIERRE AUGUSTE RENOIR, French, 1841–1919
Museum of Fine Arts, Boston. Oil on canvas, 71 1/2 x 36 1/2 in.

The Lovers in the Country, Sentiments of Youth, Paris, after 1844
GUSTAVE COURBET (attributed), French, 1819–1877
Musée du Petit Palais, Paris. Oil on canvas, 23 3/4 x 19 1/2 in.

♣ Notes and Nosegays

Surprised as she slips a love note into a bouquet of flowers, the young woman in Jean-Honoré Fragonard's *The Love Letter* turns to give the viewer a piquant glance. Her face, caught in the radiant light from the window, is the brightest and most carefully finished area of the painting. Fragonard's superb technical facility is evident in the brilliant brushwork of the girl's fashionable blue dress and in the freely painted outer edges of the picture. The leg of the desk has been rendered in transparent ocher underpainting, and the silky ears of the little lapdog have been described in squiggles of white paint. The inscription on the note, "A Monsieur Mon Cuviller" has given rise to differing interpretations. Some people identify the sitter as Fragonard's daughter Marie Emilie, who married her father's friend, the architect Cuviller, in 1773, after the death of her first husband. Others think that the inscription simply refers to the girl's cavalier.

In *The Bunch of Violets*, Manet's concise and elegant little painting of flowers, a note, and a fan (pages 30–31) was given as a courtly tribute and a token of friendship to Berthe Morisot, an artist who exhibited with the Impressionists and who married Manet's brother Eugène in 1874. Morisot

The Love Letter, 1770s
JEAN-HONORE FRAGONARD, French, 1732–1806
The Metropolitan Museum of Art, New York, The Jules Bache Collection, 1949. Oil on canvas, 32¾ x 26⅜ in.

DETAIL
The Love Letter

had recently posed for a portrait by Manet wearing a similar nosegay of violets as a corsage, and the painting may have been intended as a gesture of thanks. The fan, with its red lacquer guard, appears frequently in Manet's portraits of Morisot, and the note is inscribed to her. Distilled from her portraits, the younger artist's attributes have here taken on a life of their own and are presented as a graceful summation of her elegance, refinement, and distinction.

The Bunch of Violets, 1872
EDOUARD MANET, French, 1832–1883
Private collection, Paris. Oil on canvas $8^{3}/_{4}$ x $10^{3}/_{4}$ in.

Letters and Love Poems

In Suzuki Harunobu's *Young Couple,* two sweethearts bend gracefully toward one another as they examine a love letter of epic length. Rather incongruously, the young woman has the handle of a broom in her tiny hand. The composition of this print imitates Zen images of a pair of Chinese monks, Kanzan, a poet, and Jittoku, who were traditionally represented together, holding a scroll and a broom. Pastiches of this sort were not uncommon in *ukiyo-e* prints, where fashionable maidens playfully adopted the poses and attributes of ascetics, monks, and sages. The boldly carved background pattern of this woodblock print has been designed to imitate a type of marbled paper that was made by dipping the sheet quickly into a vat of water containing several separate strata of inks.

Bent double in an agony of self-conscious anticipation, the young poet in William Mulready's painting *The Sonnet* awaits his girlfriend's verdict on the poem he has just given her. Oblivious to his anxiety, she concentrates intensely on the poem itself, holding the back of her hand across her mouth in an unconsciously homely gesture of rapt absorption. Mulready was born in Ireland, but trained in London, where he taught at the Royal Academy. The technical qualities of Mulready's painting made a strong impression on his students. These included a group of young painters called the Pre-Raphaelites, who adopted his bright palette and painstaking technique and combined it with their admiration for literary and historical subjects. Departing from the usual practice of applying a warm, unifying undercolor on the surface to be painted, Mulready applied his pigments very thinly over a white ground. As a result, the artist's high-keyed, slightly acid colors have a brilliant, jewel-like quality. Mulready painted with a meticulous attention to detail. Each pebble at the edge of the stream in the foreground has been rendered individually, and the lines of the picture's initial drawing are visible in places through the thinly applied paint.

FOLLOWING PAGES: DETAIL
Young Couple

Young Couple, late 1760s
SUZUKI HARUNOBU, Japanese, c. 1725–1770
Musée Guimet, Paris. Woodblock print, $11^1/_2$ x $7^1/_2$ in.

The Sonnet, exhibited 1839
WILLIAM MULREADY, Irish, 1786–1863
Victoria and Albert Museum, London, Sheepshanks Gift. Oil on panel, $13^5/_8$ x $11^3/_4$ in.

♣ *The Stolen Kiss*

Leaning through a door, a very young man lightly grasps the wrist of a girl who has entered a room to fetch a shawl. She leans willingly toward him as he plants a delicate kiss on her cheek, but rolls her eyes anxiously toward the open door at the right, as though in fear of discovery by the cardplayers in the next room.

In Jean-Honoré Fragonard's *The Stolen Kiss*, the girl's fair coloring and white satin dress are thrown into relief against the shadowy background, and her posture and expression lend the picture an air of dramatic immediacy that contrasts amusingly with the innocence of the incident portrayed. The viewer's sense of a captured moment is reinforced by the tilt of the girl's figure and by the long, continuous line of her outstretched arm and the trailing shawl.

This picture was painted late in Fragonard's career, and the unusually meticulous rendering of surfaces such as the shining, carefully painted satin of the girl's skirt have led some scholars to suggest that the painting may have been at least partially the work of Marguerite Gérard, Fragonard's pupil and sister-in-law, who collaborated with the artist on other paintings. Whether or not this was the case, the shimmering satin also reflects a rising interest in 17th-century Dutch masters such as Gerard ter Borch among French patrons at the close of the 18th century. It is also a reminder that the painterly exuberance of Fragonard's rococo style would soon be eclipsed among fashionable patrons by the more carefully controlled draftsmanship of neoclassical artists such as Jacques-Louis David, who began their rise to prominence in the 1780s.

The Stolen Kiss, 1780s

JEAN-HONORE FRAGONARD, French, 1732–1806

Hermitage, Leningrad. Oil on canvas, 17 1/2 x 21 1/2 in.

♣ *Love Serenades*

If music be the food of love, play on," wrote William Shakespeare at the start of *Twelfth Night*. Countless works of art attest to the close relationship that has been drawn since antiquity between love and music.

In *Woman Playing a Theorbo*, Gerard ter Borch depicts a young couple leaning toward one another as though drawn together magnetically by the power of the girl's music. She is playing a theorbo, a double-necked lute, and she looks up from the music book before her to cast a soulful glance at her companion. Seated casually on a carpet-covered table, the young soldier bends forward to gaze down at her. The hat on his knee and the beribboned pocket watch on the table suggest that the moment of departure is drawing near, and their reluctance to part from one another may account for the couple's quiet intensity. Ter Borch is notable among 17th-century Dutch painters for the delicacy of his female figures and for his glittering depiction of white satin, which can be seen on the girl's skirt. The blue of her ermine-trimmed jacket and the watch ribbon stand out from the warm tones of the painting as a whole.

In Suzuki Harunobu's *Two Lovers Playing a Samisen*, the graceful figures share the playing of a single instrument, a theme with erotic overtones in Japanese art. The young woman strikes the notes with a plectrum while her lover fingers the strings. They are seated on a low bamboo bench in front of a stream with irises growing on its banks. The young woman wears a purple kimono with a knot pattern and has kicked off one of her high wooden *geta* to sit crosslegged, leaning backward against her companion. The delicately drawn faces of the pair are framed by the curving ripples of the water behind them. With great subtlety, Harunobu has used a single serpentine line to describe the water's edge, seen from above, and the raised banks that cut off the view of the iris clumps at each edge of the print. The flowing curves of the river and of the couple's garments suggest a melodic visual counterpoint to the couple's duet.

Woman Playing the Theorbo, c. 1658
GERARD TER BORCH, Dutch, 1617–1681
The Metropolitan Museum of Art, New York, Bequest of Benjamin Altman, 1913. Oil on wood, 14 1/2 x 12 3/4 in.

Two Lovers Playing a Samisen,
c. 1776–1777
SUZUKI HARUNOBU, Japanese, c. 1725–1770
Minneapolis Institute of Art, Bequest of Richard P. Gale. Woodblock print, 10 3/4 x 7 3/4 in.

Music and Love

As in song, the romances represented in art through musical metaphors may be hopeful or melancholy. Each of the two paintings reproduced here was completed late in the career of a short-lived artist. The first presents the viewer with an invitation to love; the second with a musical summation of its sorrows.

Jan Vermeer's *A Young Woman Standing at a Virginal* belongs to a large group of 17th-century Dutch pictures showing young women playing musical instruments while looking invitingly out at the viewer. In many such paintings, a second instrument awaits its player. The relationship between musical harmony and love, which is stated more obviously in other pictures, is suggested in *A Young Woman Standing at a Virginal* by a painting in the background of a cupid holding up a card. The picture within a picture conveys the symbolic message that perfect love consists of faithfulness to a single lover. Fingering the keyboard of a virginal with a painted lid, the young woman favors the viewer with an expectant but slightly enigmatic gaze. This picture shows the harmonious composition and brilliant rendering of light that distinguish Vermeer's work. Subtly arranged rectangular forms frame the standing figure, and their rhythm of verticals and horizontals is accented by the diagonal lines of the woman's arms, the back of the chair, the top of the instrument, and the shadows cast along the wall below the windowsill. The daylight that enters through the window highlights the inner edge of the ebony picture frame and sparkles on the gilt frame of the small painting. The luminosity of the woman's curls, her pearl necklace, and the ribbons of her elaborate sleeve add a lyrical intensity to an everyday subject.

Antoine Watteau's *Mezzetin* presents the viewer with a melancholy and poetic image of unrequited love. The musician in the foreground is Mezzetin, a stock character in the commedia dell'arte, a form of Italian improvisational theatre that enjoyed widespread popularity in 18th-century France. Mezzetin, whose name means "half measure," was a gentleman's servant in striped livery who served as a confidential go-between in the affairs of the gentry and who was prone to the pursuit of unsuccessful love affairs. In Watteau's rendering of the subject, he is seated on a bench in a shaded garden, pouring forth his ardor in a song. The statue of a woman, which is turned away from him in the background, hints at the outcome of his serenade; it will fall on the deaf ears of a woman made of stone. The painting may represent a stage scene or an actual one. If it is the former, the landscape and the statue so convincingly portrayed are only a painted backdrop. This layering of illusion and the creation of an ambiguous relationship between the real and the imaginary occurs often in Watteau's work. Whether the painting represents a performance or an actual love serenade, the intensity of the musician and the beautifully painted landscape lend the picture a poignant and lyrical quality.

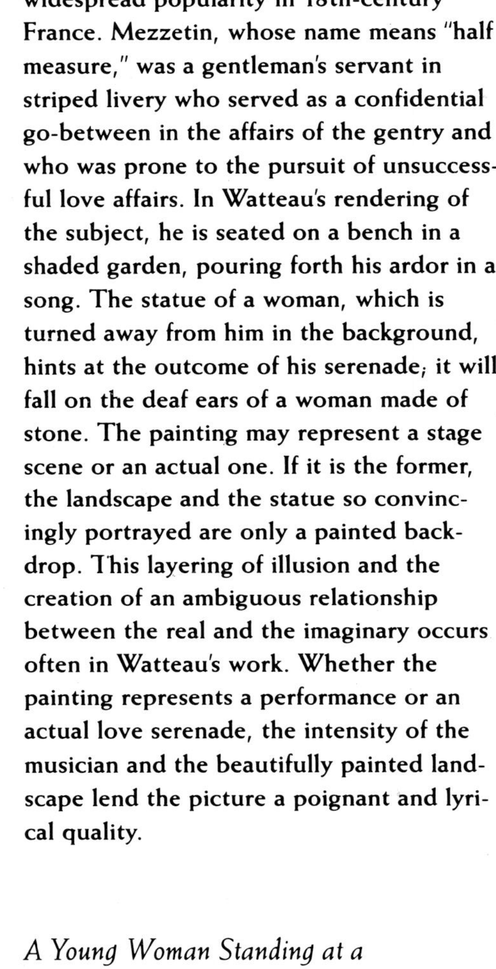

A Young Woman Standing at a Virginal, 1670s
JAN VERMEER, Dutch, 1632–1675
The National Gallery, London. Oil on canvas, $20^{1}/_{4}$ x $17^{5}/_{8}$ in.

Mezzetin, c. 1719
JEAN ANTOINE WATTEAU, French, 1684–1721
The Metropolitan Museum of Art, New York, Munsey Fund, 1934. Oil on canvas, $21^{3}/_{4}$ x 17 in.

FOLLOWING PAGES: DETAIL
Mezzetin

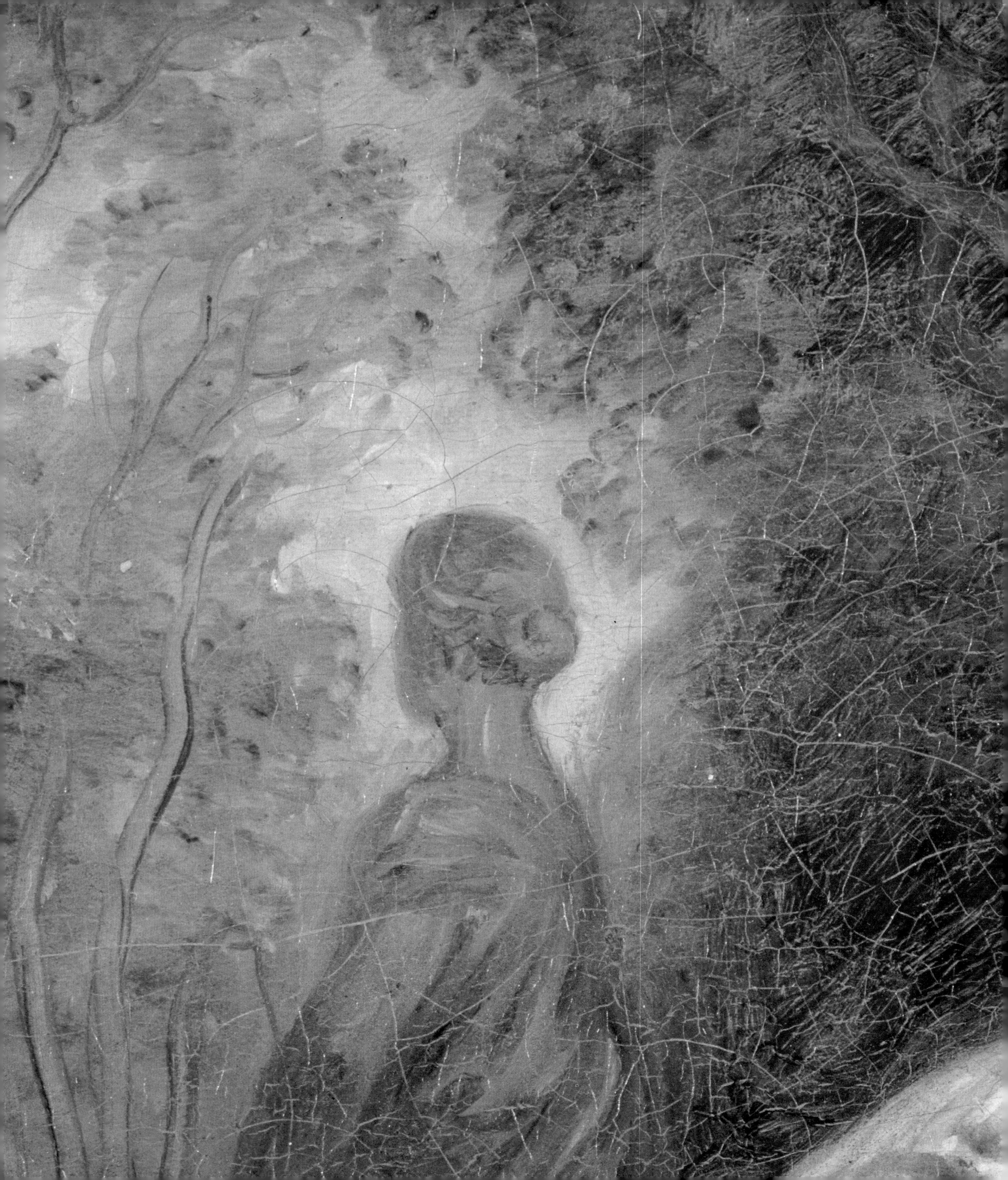

♣ In the Park

Here are two couples strolling in park settings. Each of these canvases has been painted in a restrained palette of closely related colors, and each artist has set off his figures against a large expanse of empty space in the foreground, a compositional device that probably reflected an admiration of Japanese art.

In *Public Garden with Couple and Blue Fir Tree: Poet's Garden III*, Vincent van Gogh's lovers are walking in a park in Arles, in the south of France, where van Gogh lived in 1888 and 1889. At the time, he was renting a yellow house on the Place Lamartine and awaiting the arrival of his friend and fellow-artist Paul Gauguin, who shared the house with him for two months in the autumn of 1888. This picture was one of a series of four canvases entitled *The Poet's Garden* that van Gogh painted to decorate Gauguin's bedroom in the yellow house. Van Gogh sent a sketch of this painting to his brother Theo in a letter, adding, "Imagine an immense pine tree of greenish blue, spreading its branches horizontally over a bright green lawn, and gravel splashed with light and shade. Two figures of lovers in the shade of the great tree. . .This very simple patch of garden is brightened by beds of geraniums, orange in the distance under black branches."

The woman wears the characteristic black dress of the Arlésienne, and the man's straw hat is similar to one that van Gogh wore in a self-portrait painted shortly before his departure for Arles. He associated the straw hat with the older Provençal artist Adolphe Monticelli, whom he greatly admired. Van Gogh's personal identification with Monticelli is suggested in a letter in which he compared the artist to the

Public Garden with Couple and Blue Fir Tree: Poet's Garden III, 1888
VINCENT VAN GOGH, Dutch, 1853–1890
Private Collection. Oil on canvas, 28¾ x 36¼ in.

medieval writer Boccaccio as "a melancholic, somewhat resigned, unhappy man who saw the wedding party of the world pass by, painting and analyzing the lovers of his time—he, the one who had been left out of things."

In John Singer Sargent's *Luxembourg Gardens at Twilight*, a couple is walking at dusk in the Paris park. The rising moon and the dome of the Pantheon are visible above the trees. The quiet, luminous colors of the painting evoke the peaceful mood of twilight. Born in Florence, Italy, to American parents living abroad, the cosmopolitan Sargent studied in Florence and Rome before coming to Paris to study with the successful academic painter Emile Auguste Carolus-Duran. Sargent was still in his early twenties when he painted this picture.

Luxembourg Gardens at Twilight, c. 1879

JOHN SINGER SARGENT, American, 1856–1925

Minneapolis Institute of Arts, Gift of Mrs. C. C. Bovey and Mrs. C. D. Velie. Oil on canvas, 29 x 36 1/2 in.

to my friend McKim. John S. Sargent

♣ Moonlight

*M*an and Woman Contemplating the Moon, by Caspar David Friedrich, conveys a sense of mysterious intensity. Standing on a steep path, a couple gazes at the full moon, the woman leaning slightly on the man as though for support. Above them are the drooping needles of a giant pine tree, and beside them, a huge dead oak tree leans into an abyss, its partially torn roots silhouetted strangely against the moonlit sky. The couple represented are probably the artist and his wife Caroline.

A German Romantic painter, Friedrich approached landscape in a visionary and often symbolic manner, expressing his sense of the vastness of nature and the relative insignificance of humanity in comparison to the harmony and power of the natural world. Often his paintings contain Christian symbolism, and in this painting, it is likely that the dead oak symbolizes paganism while the evergreen pine represents Christianity. The primeval rock near the oak tree underscores its association with pre-Christian religion, because it was copied from a sketch of a prehistoric monument that Friedrich had made in 1806. The painting has Friedrich's characteristic meticulous finish, giving the impression that the landscape has been described without the intervention of the artist's hand. The twisted, expressive tracery of the oak tree is reminiscent of Albrecht Dürer's engravings and other German work of the 15th and 16th centuries. German Romantic artists at the beginning of the 19th century had rediscovered the art of their predecessors and adopted it as their artistic heritage.

Man and Woman Contemplating the Moon,
c. 1830–1835
CASPAR DAVID FRIEDRICH, German, 1774–1840
Nationalgalerie, Berlin. Oil on canvas, 13¼ x 17 ⅛ in.

35. Un Seigneur Mahometan avec une femme quil embrasse

♣ A Fond Embrace

Surely the 18th-century Indian miniature *Lovers at the Window* conveys the sentiment expressed in the lines from Ben Jonson's poem *To Celia*: "Drink to me, only, with thine eyes / And I will pledge with mine; / Or leave a kiss but in the cup, / And I'll not look for wine."

Nose to nose, the figures in the miniature stare raptly into one another's huge, dark eyes, ignoring the tiny cup that the man holds between them. His arm is wrapped protectively around his lover, and the complex rhythm of the couple's hands and arms is accentuated by the serpentine windings of the woman's drapery. The influence of Persian court art in India during this time is evident in the delicate floral tracery on the colorful borders of the image.

In *Lovers in a Garden*, Hishikawa Moronobu's young man reaches out to hug his shy companion. The couple is partially screened behind a delicate tracery of chrysanthemums and autumn grasses, but the viewer's eye is drawn to the bold black patterning of their hair and the girl's kimono. The curves of their embracing figures are echoed in the sinuous lines of the stream and the weathered rock in the background, conveying the couple's harmony with their natural surroundings. This gently romantic scene was probably the frontispiece for an album of erotic prints, which were known as *shunga*.

Moronobu was the first great pioneer of *ukiyo-e* printmaking, and his black-and-white, single-sheet woodblock prints shaped a tradition that remained popular for over 200 years. For several centuries, woodblocks had been used in Japan for the printing and illustration of books, but it was not until Moronobu's time that they became an important means of producing independent works of art.

Lovers at the Window

INDIAN, Jaipur, early 18th century

Islamisches Museum der Staatliche Museen du Berlin. Body color on paper, 5 1/4 x 8 1/4 in.

Lovers in a Garden, c. *1676–1683*

HISHIKAWA KICHIBEI MORONOBU, Japanese, 1625–1694

The Metropolitan Museum of Art, New York, Harris Brisbane Dick Fund. Woodblock print, 9 1/4 x 13 1/4 in.

Lovers Embracing

The Lovers, 1923
PABLO PICASSO, Spanish, 1881–1973
National Gallery of Art, Washington, D.C. Oil on canvas, 51 1/4 x 38 1/4 in.

Pablo Picasso's *The Lovers* dates from 1923. Some of the artist's paintings from this period continue the cubist experimentation of his earlier work, while others, like this one, reveal Picasso's deep involvement in the art of classical antiquity. This interest had been rekindled by the artist's visit to Rome in 1917, where he worked with Jean Cocteau on the ballet *Parade* and met the ballerina Olga Koklova, whom he married in 1918. On his return home to Paris, he painted a series of works inspired by ancient sculpture and Greek vase painting. In *The Lovers*, the man and woman touch one another lightly and tenderly. They have been drawn in very simple outlines, and their forms have been painted in flat, translucent colors with very little shading. Their delicate faces have the straight-nosed features of classical Greek sculpture.

Peleus Clasping Thetis shows a moment of struggle in the courting of Thetis by the mortal Peleus. Because the sea-nymph had refused to marry a mortal, Peleus was forced to win her by wrestling; here he clasps the elusive nymph as she tries to evade him by changing her form, appearing first as a lion and then as a serpent. The force of Peleus' grip can be seen in his interlocked fingers, which echo the pattern of the Greek key, or *meander*, that forms a circular border around the figures. Peleus won his bride, who later became the mother of the hero Achilles. This painting, from the inside of a *kylix*, or flat, stemmed drinking cup, is decorated in a technique known as red-figure. In contrast to earlier Greek pottery, where the figures were painted in an iron-rich clay that turned black when fired, the couple here has been drawn with black outlines on the red body of the vase, and the area around them has been painted.

Peleus Clasping Thetis, from a kylix (wine cup), c. 500 B.C.
PEITHINOS, Greek, late 6th century B.C.
Antikenmuseum, Staatliche Museen Preussischer Kulturbesitz, Berlin. Pottery, 13 3/4 in. diameter.

❧ Reflections of Love

In the painting *Allegory*, by a follower of the 16th-century Venetian painter Titian, two lovers stand in the foreground in a pose that resembles, in reverse, the embrace of Picasso's lovers on page 52. The man holds up a mirror into which the woman gazes demurely, while presenting the splendor of her nude torso and golden tresses to the viewer. Her finger is placed on the mouth of a perfume bottle and a gold ring lies next to it in the foreground. The picture is based closely on a painting of two clothed lovers by Titian, but the allegorical meaning of both works is unclear. Mirrors are often associated with vanity and the transience of earthly pleasures, and this may be the meaning suggested here. Even if this is the case, the artist has celebrated the visual delight of the physical world, rendering the rich textures of flesh, hair, cloth, and glass with the sumptuous brushwork typical of Venetian Renaissance painting.

The contemporary American artist Roy Lichtenstein, a founder of the movement known as Pop Art, has always been interested in popular culture, and has used comic books, newspaper advertisements, and other images drawn from the mass media as sources for his art. Since the mid-1960s he has also quoted from art history in his work. *Stepping Out*, painted in 1978, unites the restricted color palette of the 20th-century Dutch artist Piet Mondrian with the Benday dots of comic-book printing, and combines popular imagery with references to the work of the 20th-century French painter Fernand Léger. The dapper young man is borrowed from a figure in a Léger painting, while his female companion combines popular and artistic elements. The startling rearrangement of her features recalls surrealist art of the 1920s and 1930s, but the features themselves, the full lips, mascara-laden eyelashes, and Bardot-like blonde tresses and scarf echo popular fashion of the 1960s. Amusingly, the woman's face is constructed on a mirror, so that she is presented to the viewer as a literal reflection of contemporary, media-influenced notions of glamour.

Allegory
FOLLOWER OF TIZIANO VECELLIO, CALLED TITIAN, 16th century.
National Gallery of Art, Washington, D.C., Samuel Kress Collection. Oil on canvas, 36 x 32¼ in.

Stepping Out, 1978
ROY LICHTENSTEIN, American, 1923–
The Metropolitan Museum of Art, New York, Purchase Lila Acheson Wallace Gift, Arthur Hoppock Hearn Fund, Arthur Lejwa Fund in honor of Jean Arp, the Bernhill Fund, Joseph H. Hazen Foundation, Inc., Samuel I. Newhouse Foundation, Inc., Walter Bareiss, Marie Bannon McHenry, Louis Smith and Stephen C. Swid Gifts, 1980. Oil and magna on canvas, 86 x 70 in.

FOLLOWING PAGES: DETAIL
Allegory

♣ *Love Triumphant*

The two images illustrated here represent triumphant couples in outdoor settings. Each work formed part of a larger group of decorations for a noble residence.

In the 15th-century tapestry *Lady and Gentleman in Front of a Tent*, an elegantly dressed couple stands in a flower-strewn meadow as angels behind them hold open the curtains of a crowned canopy. The woman is watering a container of flowers, while at the man's feet, a tiny but ferocious-looking dog prepares to gnaw a bone. Tapestries representing courtly groups enjoying the country pleasures of hunting, hawking, dancing, music, and outdoor games were popular among the nobility in the 15th and 16th centuries, and workshops in France and Flanders catered to the demand for such works to decorate large châteaux. Often these were made in sets, called "chambers," to ornament a room or a hall. Woven from wool, they insulated the castle's inhabitants from the damp chill of stone walls, and their colorful subjects must have brightened the gloom of many medieval winters.

Fragonard's *The Lover Crowned* forms part of a group of 14 canvases that were commissioned by Madame du Barry, the mistress of Louis XV, for her château at Louveciennes, a gift of the king. Together with smaller panels representing flowers and cupids, four large scenes depicted incidents from the progress of love: *The Meeting*, *The Pursuit*, *The Lover Crowned*, and *Love Letters*. *The Lover Crowned* is the third of the four paintings. In it, a young woman is seated below a statue of a reclining cupid in a shady garden, holding a flowered crown over the head of the admiring lover at her feet. Amid a profusion of blossoms in the foreground, an artist sketches the happy couple. Fragonard seems to have intended his quartet of paintings as isolated scenes rather than as a narrative sequence. Madame du Barry, who had completed an ambitious redecoration of the Château de Louveciennes and commissioned a strikingly modern country house, apparently felt that Fragonard's paintings were too old-fashioned to suit her, and she rejected them in favor of a more up-to-date set of pictures by the neoclassical painter Joseph-Marie Vien. Fragonard kept the paintings, and installed them in the house of his cousin at Grasse. They are now on view together at the Frick Collection in New York.

Lady and Gentleman In Front of a Tent, *c. 1460–1465.*
TOURNAI OR BRUSSELS
Musée des Arts Décoratifs, Paris. Tapestry, 95 1/2 x 74 3/4 in.

The Lover Crowned, c. 1772
JEAN-HONORE FRAGONARD, French, 1732–1806
The Frick Collection, New York. Oil on canvas, 125 1/8 x 95 3/4 in.

Passion

The moth's kiss, first!
Kiss me as if you made believe
You were not sure, this eve,
How my face, your flower, had pursed
Its petals up; so, here and there
You brush it, till I grow aware
Who wants me, and wide ope I burst.

The bee's kiss, now!
Kiss me as if you entered gay
My heart at some noonday,
A bud that dares not disallow
The claim, so all is rendered up,
And passively its shattered cup
Over your head to sleep I bow.

ROBERT BROWNING
from **In a Gondola**

❧ *The Kiss*

In *The Kiss*, Edvard Munch's embracing figures fuse together into a single, serpentine form, with their intertwined arms looping gracefully around their joined faces. Their black garments form a single silhouette against the wood grain of the print's background, emphasizing their unity.

The Norwegian artist Munch arrived in Paris in 1889, where he was strongly influenced by the work of Vincent van Gogh and Paul Gauguin, and by the symbolist movement. This literary and artistic movement, developed by a group that included the poet Stéphane Mallarmé and the artists Gustave Moreau and Odilon Redon, was based on the theory that art should suggest ideas and emotions through the use of symbols rather than attempt to depict an objective reality. This subjective and emotionally charged means of expression coincided with Munch's interest in the themes of love and death.

In 1892, Munch completed a painting of *The Kiss*. During that year, he also began a series of experimental prints, in which he reworked the theme of the kiss repeatedly. The final versions of this image occurred in the starkly simplified woodcuts of 1902, one of which is illustrated here. Munch's use of flat, uncarved areas of wood grain in his prints showed his awareness of Japanese prints and his admiration for the woodcuts of Paul Gauguin, whose daring experimentation in the 1890s changed the course of woodblock printmaking in France. Munch also showed a willingness to try technical innovations, sometimes cutting apart his woodblocks with a jigsaw so that he could ink the colors of each area separately and reassemble them for printing.

Lovers kissing was a favorite theme of the Romanian sculptor Constantin Brancusi, and at least six other variations of the subject exist, including an earlier, more naturalistic version that serves as a gravestone in the Montparnasse Cemetery in Paris. In the version illustrated here, the figures are united in the unbroken form of the limestone block. They are presented as equals, embracing eye to eye. Only the woman's gently rounded breasts and longer hair distinguish her from her companion. The abstract simplicity of the couple reflects Brancusi's interest in the African sculpture collected by other artists living in Paris, as well as his attachment to his Romanian peasant heritage, with its tradition of simplified carved forms and its craftsmanlike delight in materials. The severely formal reduction of the figures made this a startlingly modern work in 1912, and yet, pressed together in a close embrace, the couple conveys a sense of tenderness and permanence.

The Kiss, 1912
CONSTANTIN BRANCUSI, Romanian, 1876–1957
The Philadelphia Museum of Art, Louise and Walter Arensberg Collection. Limestone, 23 x 13 in.

The Kiss, 1902
EDVARD MUNCH, Norwegian, 1863–1944
National Gallery of Art, Washington, D.C., The Sarah G. and Lionel C. Epstein Family Collection. Woodcut, printed from two blocks in black and gray on brown paper, $18^{1}/_{2}$ x $17^{3}/_{4}$ in.

Lovers, 1920
PAUL KLEE, Swiss, 1879–1940
The Metropolitan Museum of Art, New York, The Berggruen Klee Collection, 1987. Gouache and pencil on paper, 9¾ x 16 in.

❧ *A Lovers' Embrace*

Paul Klee's *Lovers* is a good example of the delicacy, mystery, and wit of the Swiss artist's work. The full title of this small piece, recorded in Klee's catalogue of works, is *Lovers, Erotic Watercolor in Monumental Style*. Klee's treatment of sexuality is usually ironic, and often the content of his erotic works can be ascertained more readily from their titles than from the images themselves. This piece, painted in an opaque watercolor medium known as gouache, shows a pair of lovers set against a background of red and black bands that continue into the figures themselves. At the left a man appears to be in ardent pursuit of his companion, who waves an outstretched arm. The couple's large round eyes stare outward at the viewer, and the man has a third eye set oddly into his body. The lovers' garments are rendered by a whimsical pattern of small diamonds. The watercolor has been pasted onto a piece of black cardboard in an asymmetrical fashion, so that the couple is placed in the center of the composition.

Reza-ye 'Abbasi's *Courtly Lovers* are intertwined in a languorous pose; the woman leans backward and arches her torso as her companion slips his hand into her open robe. In the foreground of the miniature is a delicately painted still life of fruit and wine. Reza-ye 'Abbasi was a court artist for the Persian Safavid dynasty in the early 17th century. When he became the favorite painter of the Sultan Shah Abbas, he changed his signature from Aqa Reza to Reza-ye 'Abbasi. Reza had been trained in the royal workshops, but departed from the tradition of his teachers to develop a fluid, calligraphic style. This innovation suited the changing taste of his patrons, who were turning away from elaborately illustrated manuscripts in favor of single drawings and miniatures that could be collected into albums. In contrast to the brightly colored complexity of earlier miniatures, *Courtly Lovers* presents two large figures isolated against a monochrome ground. The sensuous lines of their intertwined bodies are framed by the ornamental landscape, with its calligraphic tracery of golden leaves, branches, and clouds.

Courtly Lovers, 1630

REZA–YE 'ABBASI, Iranian

The Metropolitan Museum of Art, New York, Francis M. Weld Fund, 1950. Opaque watercolor, ink, and gold on paper, 7 1/8 x 4 11/16 in.

❧ Passionate Embrace

In *The Kiss*, Gustav Klimt's embracing figures are painted on a gold background reminiscent of Byzantine icons. They are surrounded by a golden halo and united in a mass of richly ornamented gold cloth that suggests a religious exaltation of the image of love, and yet their relationship remains somewhat ambiguous. The man leans ardently over the woman, holding her head in both of his hands. She turns her face to the side, offering her cheek to his kiss. Her clenched hand on his shoulder, closed eyes, and tensed feet could indicate either excitement or silent resistance. She is kneeling on a flowery meadow that drops away into a precipice at the right, suggesting possible danger for the lovers. Her feet, braced against its edge, are garlanded with long chains of gold, and tiny flowers scattered in her hair give the effect of a halo. The man's voluminous robe, decorated with rectangular shapes, conceals his body, and it is difficult to guess whether he is kneeling or standing. His muscular shoulders and forceful gestures convey his dominance, and the woman's compressed posture and mask-like expression suggest a passivity whose emotional content is difficult to read.

In Paul Gauguin's woodcut, *Te Faruru*, a Tahitian couple is locked in a mysterious and passionate embrace. The contours of their figures, illuminated by the firelight in the background, seem to flicker in the darkness. The woman's contorted pose conveys a mood of sensual abandon. Twisting her torso and bracing her elongated hand against the ground, she leans backward against her lover's arm so that her inverted features are visible. Behind the couple is the sinuous form of the leaping flames, and above the man's head, the profile of a spirit is visible in the firelight.

This was one of a series of ten woodcuts that Gauguin made in Paris after returning from his first stay in Tahiti. They were created to illustrate *Noa Noa* (Fragrance), a book that the artist wrote about his Tahitian experiences, although they were not included in the published volume. Gauguin replaced the meticulous technique of traditional woodcuts with a restless and daring willingness to experiment in the carving of blocks and the printing of images. His contemporaries recognized the revolutionary nature of these works, which transformed woodcut printmaking in France and had a strong influence on younger artists such as Edvard Munch. In these prints, Gauguin emphasized the process of carving the block, leaving large surfaces of uncut wood, and inking the cut-away white areas to emphasize their gouge marks. Each image from this series exists in a number of variations; this example was printed twice, in different colors, from the same block and accentuated by hand coloring.

Te Faruru (Here They Love), 1893–1894

PAUL GAUGUIN, French, 1848–1903

The Art Institute of Chicago, Clarence Bunkingham Collection, 1950.158. Woodcut, printed twice from same block in black and ocher with hand coloring, 12 7/8 x 8 in.

The Kiss, 1907–1908

GUSTAV KLIMT, Austrian, 1862–1918

Osterreichische Galerie, Vienna. Oil on canvas, 70 13/16 x 70 13/16 in.

FOLLOWING PAGES: DETAIL
The Kiss

Bonnard
1900

❧ In a Bedroom

In *Prince Murad Baksh Receiving a Lady at Night*, the young Mughal nobleman, who has evidently sent for a companion, looks up eagerly as she appears between two attendants. With becoming modesty—or perhaps nervousness—she clasps the hand of one of her guides and grips the veil of the other. Still wearing his headdress, the young prince reclines on a canopied bed, whose rope supports have been depicted in an improbable manner in order to avoid obscuring the foreground figures. The bed has been set up on an outdoor terrace, perhaps to catch the evening breeze, and an attendant holding a fan stands behind the prince. Beyond the terrace, boats float on a body of water before a white palace, and a cluster of buildings is dimly visible behind the prince's head. The sky is spangled with stars, and a crescent moon is visible at the upper right.

In Pierre Bonnard's *Man and Woman*, a young woman in a lamplit room reclines on a bed in a relaxed, feline pose. She is absorbed in playing with a pair of kittens. At the right of a folded screen that divides the painting, a man stands dressing or undressing, his face in shadow. The figures represent the artist and his lifelong companion Marthe de Méligny, but the picture is less a double portrait than a generalized representation of a couple. The painting's direct eroticism and its representation of a male figure is unusual in Bonnard's work, which was primarily devoted in later years to solitary nudes and domestic scenes. The psychological isolation of these two figures suggests that Bonnard was interested in the art of the Norwegian artist Edvard Munch, whose work had been shown in Paris during the decade prior to the painting of this picture.

Prince Murad Baksh Receiving a Lady at Night, 1680–1690
INDIAN, Mughal, late 17th century
Victoria and Albert Museum, London. Guoache on paper, 12 7/8 x 17 3/8 in.

Man and Woman, 1900
PIERRE BONNARD, French, 1867–1947
Musée d'Orsay, Paris. Oil on canvas, 45 1/4 x 28 1/2 in.

❧ *In Bed*

The man and the woman in Kitagawa Utamaro's *Lovers* survey one another in a close-up view, their faces pressed together in a moment of passion. The man's staring eye is visible beside his companion's carefully arranged hair, and each figure's field of vision is filled with the face of the other. The woman's hand caresses her companion's face, and his fingers grip the nape of her neck, which in 18th century Japan was considered to be one of the most beautiful and seductive parts of the female body. Her leg is covered with a translucent veil of dotted cloth, and the man holds an open fan inscribed with an erotic poem. The man is thought by some scholars to be a self-portrait by Utamaro, since the artist portrayed himself in another print wearing the same kimono.

Lovers was one of 12 woodblock prints from a series entitled *The Poem of the Pillow* that launched the 34-year-old Utamaro into prominence as one of the foremost *ukiyo-e* printmakers of the late 18th century. Renowned for his treatment of women and erotic subjects, he was one of the first Japanese printmakers to come to the attention of 19th-century French artists. Like many of his predecessors, Utamaro depicted the world of courtesans and their admirers, but his work achieved a unique combination of psychological insight and sensuous appeal. His wide-ranging studies of women of various social classes at work and at play broadened the subject matter of Japanese printmaking.

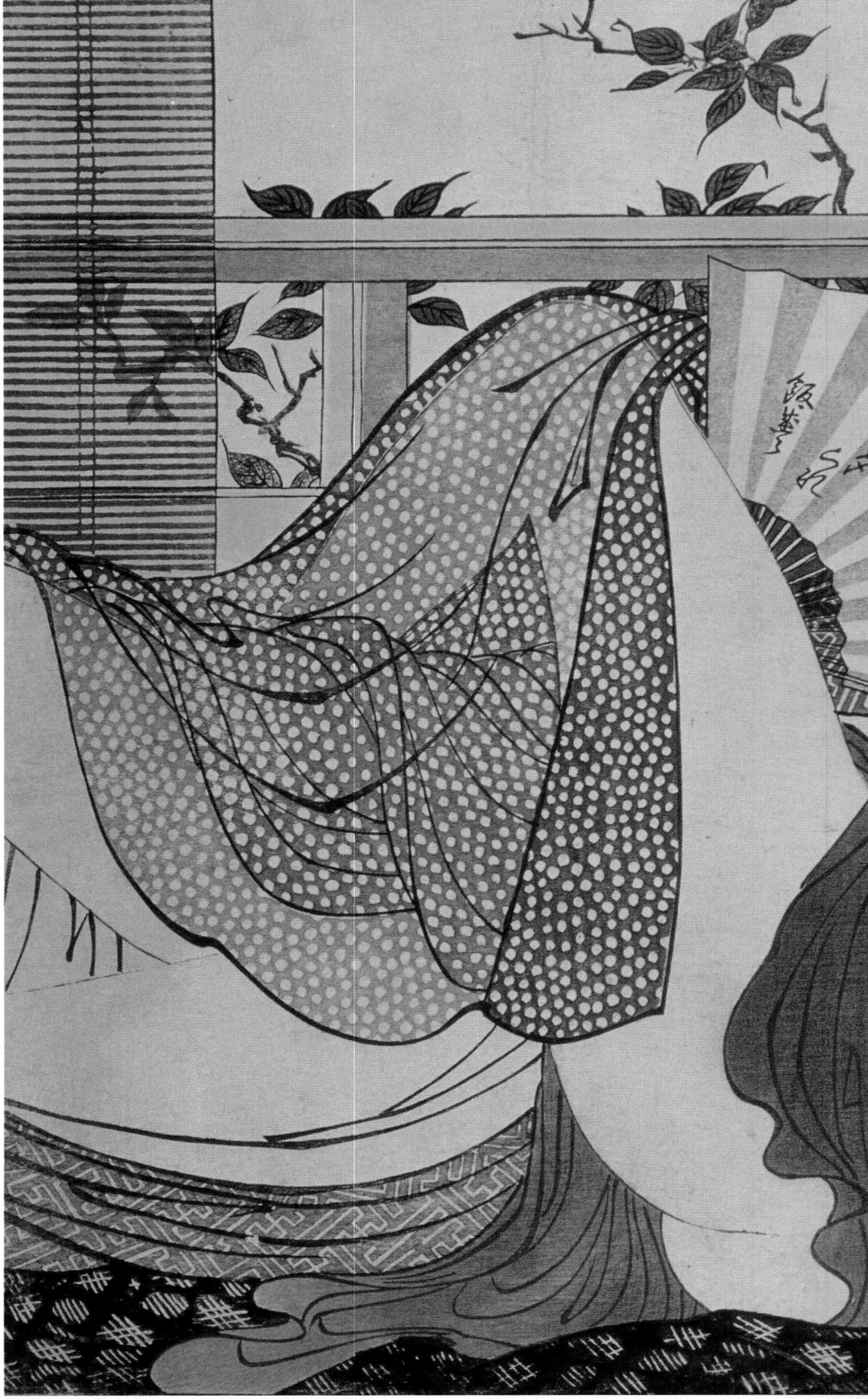

Lovers from *The Poem of The Pillow*, 1788

KITAGAWA UTAMARO, Japanese, 1753–1806

Victoria and Albert Museum, London. Woodblock print, 10 x 15 in.

Lovers Under a Mosquito Net
ISODA KORYUSAI, Japanese, active mid-1760s–1780s
Private Collection. Woodblock print.

Moments of Passion

In the side of the red terra cotta vase illustrated here, two lovers embrace in a moment of delicate erotic intimacy. Their downcast eyes, hidden in shadow, lend a dreamy expression to their faces and reinforce the emotional quality conveyed by this relief. This drinking cup dates from the early years of the Roman empire. It is of a type of manufacture called Arretine ware that was used at the parties of the wealthy.

The Romans of the early empire looked to their Greek predecessors for stylistic inspiration, and this Hellenizing taste was particularly strong during the reign of the Emperor Augustus, when much of the best Arretine ware was made. The influence of classical Greek sculpture can be seen in the profiles of these embracing lovers. Like Greek vases, which were also painted with sexual scenes for the enjoyment of party and symposium guests, Arretine ware was often decorated with erotic images. These works, however, were much more intimate and personal in feeling than the exuberantly matter-of-fact sexuality depicted by the Greeks. On this Arretine vase, other couples are represented around the sides, but each pair conveys the sense of a private and deeply felt experience.

Isoda Koryusai's *Lovers Under a Mosquito Net* depicts an amorous couple peering out from behind a mesh curtain that casts a delicate veil across their entwined bodies. Their impassive expressions contrast with their sensuous embrace and their rumpled bedclothes. The bed is surrounded by patterned screens, and nearby, on the tatami mats, are smoking implements and an ornate lacquer box. Behind the box sits a tiny female figure observing the couple in bed. Her comments appear in the inscription above her.

Isoda Koryusai, a former samurai, was a friend and pupil of Suzuki Harunobu, and many of his early compositions were based closely on the work of his master. Harunobu had produced a suite of 24 erotic prints featuring the voyeuristic adventures of a tiny man, and this print was part of a series that Koryusai designed as its sequel, with a miniature woman as its protagonist.

Arretine Vase, Late 1st century B. C.
ROMAN
Ashmolean Museum, Oxford. Terracotta, height 5¾ in.

❧ *Love Conquers War*

In Sandro Botticelli's *Venus and Mars*, the goddess of love is reclining with the god of war, who has fallen into a profound sleep. Three baby satyrs have captured his lance. One of them totters forward wearing his helmet, while another attempts to wake him with a blast from a conch-shell trumpet. A fourth satyr is wearing his cuirass. Although legend relates that Venus was married to Vulcan, the god of fire, she was also associated with several lovers, the most important of whom was Mars.

In Botticelli's work, pagan themes were treated with a dignity and seriousness that had been reserved since the Middle Ages for Christian subjects. In the early part of his career, the artist belonged to a circle of Florentine scholars and thinkers who were attempting to fuse classical art and mythology with Christian philosophy. In *Venus and Mars*, Botticelli's brilliant success at combining those two traditions can be seen in the figure of the sleeping Mars, which unites the classical proportions and pose of

Venus and Mars, c. 1483
SANDRO BOTTICELLI, Italian, c. 1445–1510
National Gallery, London. Tempera on wood, 27¼ x 68¼ in.

a Roman river god with the human pathos and vulnerability seen in Renaissance paintings of the dead Christ. In contrast to the sleeping god and the frolicking little satyrs, the alert figure of Venus communicates a sense of quiet confidence and power. Her white robe ripples and undulates with a complex, fluid motion that recalls the ebb and flow of the sea from which she was born, visible in the background. Although the exact meaning of this painting's mythological subject remains somewhat mysterious, the general intention is erotic, and the painting's overall message seems to be that love conquers war. The wasps buzzing around the head of the sleeping Mars may indicate that the picture was painted for the Vespucci family, since that species of insect (called *vespa*, in Italian) was the family's emblem. This was the family of the explorer Amerigo Vespucci (1451–1512), Botticelli's contemporary, after whom America was named.

A. Feuerbach. 1864.

❧ A Fateful Passion

The story of Paolo and Francesca is told in the fifth canto of Dante's *Inferno*. Francesca was the young wife of the ruler of Rimini, a warlike and physically unattractive man who spent a great deal of time away from his castle fighting battles. When he was away, Francesca was left with his handsome younger brother Paolo, and although they tried to remain loyal to the absent ruler, they were overpowered by the irresistible forces of youthful passion. Both of the paintings reproduced here show the decisive moment described by Dante, in which the young couple, reading a romantic account of the adventures of Lancelot, look up and discover their feelings for one another: "That day, we read no more."

Jean Auguste Dominique Ingres' *Paolo and Francesca* condenses the entire dramatic narrative into a single moment. Overcome with love, Paolo leans violently forward to kiss Francesca's cheek. She turns away modestly, but the book has fallen from her hand. Her furious husband leaps into view at the right, drawing his sword to kill the two people he loves best. Ingres was a consummate draftsman, although the proportions of his figures are sometimes surprising, as is the case in this picture. Ingres observed and re-created many of the details of Renaissance costume in this work, and his admiration for Raphael is evident in the painting of Francesca's face.

In contrast to the drama of the Ingres painting, Anselm Feuerbach's *Paolo and Francesca da Rimini* concentrates on the sentimental aspect of the story. Francesca's voluminous gown reflects Victorian taste more closely than it follows Renaissance fashion, and the two lovers create a mood of quiet, amorous charm that gives no hint of their tempestuous future.

Paolo and Francesca, 1859
JEAN-AUGUSTE-DOMINIQUE INGRES, French 1780–1867
Musée des Beaux-Arts, Angers. Oil on canvas, 19 x 15³/₈ in.

Paolo and Francesca da Rimini, 1864
ANSELM FEUERBACH, German, 1829–1880
Bayerische Staatsgemäldesammlungen, Munich. Oil on canvas, 53¹/₂ x 38³/₈ in.

❧ Infidelity

Paolo Veronese's *Infidelity* is one of four allegorical paintings on the subject of love that were intended as decorations for a palace ceiling. In this image, the monumental figure of a woman, seen from below, is placed between a bearded man and a youth. She holds the hand of one while secretly slipping a note to the other, who looks away in order to disguise the action. A surprisingly muscular infant pulls her toward the beardless man, while his winged companion looks up apprehensively. The adults probably represent Venus hesitating between Mars and Mercury, while the two children may represent Eros, the symbol of impulsive, illegitimate love, and Anteros, associated with legitimate, mutual love.

Veronese's brilliant brushwork and subtle sense of color placed him, along with Titian, at the forefront of 16th-century Venetian painting. In the canvas reproduced here, he has used several techniques for modulating the depth of the represented space by emphasizing the flat, painted nature of the image. The arching gesture of the woman's arms is echoed in the tree branches above her, and the sky has been rendered with a thinly brushed layer of blue over a reddish undercoat that shows through it, calling the viewer's attention to the texture of the canvas. Veronese's sophistication as a colorist can be seen in the harmonious chord of orange and salmon colors formed by the men's clothing, and by the subtle variations of green in the leaves, the rocky ledge, and the woman's cloak. The beautifully painted flesh of the woman is modeled by shadows and blushes, and her golden hair is accentuated by dazzling highlights.

Infidelity, 1576
PAOLO VERONESE, Italian, 1528–1588
The National Gallery, London. Oil on canvas, 74 x 74 in.

DETAIL
Infidelity

Joseph and Potiphar's Wife, c. 1555
JACOPO ROBUSTI, CALLED TINTORETTO,
Italian, 1518–1594

Museo del Prado, Madrid. Oil on canvas,
21¼ x 46 in.

❧ A Failed Seduction

Tintoretto's *Joseph and Potiphar's Wife* depicts a scene from a story told in the Old Testament book of Genesis. Joseph, purchased and brought to Egypt by Potiphar, a captain of Pharaoh's guard, had been entrusted with the management of his master's household. Potiphar's wife, attracted by the beauty of the young man, tried to seduce him, but failed. Finally, waiting until the house was empty, she seized his robe in a final attempt. Joseph fled, leaving the garment in her hands, which she used as evidence to accuse him falsely of attacking her.

In Tintoretto's painting, the sumptuous figure of Potiphar's wife is stretched diagonally across the left half of the canvas as she reaches for Joseph's clothing. Caught unexpectedly, he topples backward and turns to escape her. His unbalanced pose is accentuated by the dramatic swags of the curtains in the background. The figures are painted as if seen from below, for this canvas was one of a set of six pictures representing Old Testament scenes that were intended to form part of a ceiling decoration. The rich textures and brilliant colors of this small painting contrast with the somewhat darker and less chromatic style that Tintoretto developed later in his career.

Claiming that he wanted to combine Michelangelo's drawing with the color of Titian, the ambitious and energetic artist undertook huge commissions such as the well-known ceiling of the Scuola di San Rocco, in Venice. In these enormous works, meant to be seen from afar, he developed dynamic compositions and dramatic effects of light and shadow that lent a strong sense of emotional immediacy to his work.

The Rake's Progress: The Orgy, c. *1734*
WILLIAM HOGARTH, British, 1697–1764
Sir John Soane's Museum, London. Oil on canvas, $24^{1}/_{2}$ x $29^{1}/_{2}$ in.

Rakes and Harlots

Promiscuity and prostitution are the subjects of the works illustrated here, and yet the moods of the pictures and the attitudes of the people portrayed in them could hardly be more dissimilar. The heartless and self-indulgent young rake in William Hogarth's boisterous tavern scene has eagerly embraced the pleasures of alcohol and casual sex. In contrast, Kitagawa Utamaro's pensive prostitute is fantasizing about the rich and respectable marriage that would secure her future.

In Utamaro's *Courtesan Dreaming of Her Wedding*, a young woman leans against a small table, her face screened by the fine mesh of a fan. Under her arm lies an open book, which may have inspired the satisfying vision that appears in the balloon above her head. In it is her elegant wedding procession, which includes a closed sedan chair and a group of attendants wearing broad hats. Next to the courtesan's dream, Utamaro has placed an inset depicting a classic literary subject. This image, which presents a parallel to the larger scene, shows the Chinese scholar Rosei, who slept on a magic pillow and dreamed of wonderful events that never came to pass.

William Hogarth's *The Orgy* is one of a series of paintings called *The Rake's Progress*, which describes the downfall of a selfish and dissolute young man who squanders the fortune he has inherited from his miserly father. The painting reproduced here is the third in the series, and shows the young Tom Rakewell attending a revel in a disreputable tavern. He is drunk and sprawls in his chair with his leg thrown over the lap of a prostitute who fondles his chest. She and her companion, who wear a grotesque array of beauty patches, are stealing the young man's watch. A pregnant beggar is singing for alms at the open door, and a man is entering the room with a large pewter tray to place in the center of the table. The young prostitute who is disrobing in the foreground will presently stand on the platter to display her charms.

A Courtesan Dreaming of Her Wedding,
c. 1798–1800
KITAGAWA UTAMARO, Japanese, 1753–1806
British Museum, London. Woodblock print, 15 1/16 x 10 1/16 in.

❧ Fleeting Liaisons

In the two paintings reproduced here, the viewer is invited to take an informal look at couples whose apparent relations are less than respectable.

In *Rembrandt as the Prodigal Son*, the youthful artist has chosen to portray himself as the New Testament youth who leaves his father's house to live a life of reckless abandon. His wife Saskia, perched on his knee, turns to regard the viewer steadily, looking slightly ill at ease in her role as a chance tavern acquaintance. Rembrandt, on the other hand, plays his part as a dissolute youth with genial, if slightly self-conscious gusto. With a sword buckled to his side, and a broad-brimmed hat partially shading his youthfully round face, he raises a long glass in a cheerful toast. Flush with professional success and prosperity, which were not to last, he has contrasted his own down-to-earth energy with the more patrician reserve of his young wife.

Poised in front of a mirror, Edouard Manet's model in *Nana* also looks out at the viewer, perhaps surveying her audience for potential successors to the top-hatted man who waits patiently, cane in hand, for her to finish a leisurely toilette. Her status as a courtesan is clear from the fact that she receives a visiting gentleman in her underwear. It is further emphasized by the crane on the oriental wall decoration in the background of the picture, a reference to a Parisian slang term for prostitutes. The woman's name is borrowed from the novel *L'Assommoir*, published by Manet's friend Emile Zola. In the book, Nana, the daughter of an alcoholic laundress, began her progress toward prostitution, a career Zola

Rembrandt as the Prodigal Son,
c. 1635–1636
REMBRANDT HARMENSZ. VAN RIJN, Dutch, 1606–1669
Staatlische Kunstsammlungen, Dresden. Oil on canvas, 62¾ x 51 in.

later charted in the sequel *Nana*. Parisian artists and writers of the later 19th century were fascinated by the "half-world" of female prostitution and represented the various gradations of its social scale, from the poised assurance of Manet's courtesans to the grotesque homeliness of Degas' brothel scenes. In addition to gratifying the artists' interest in forthright depictions of contemporary life, courtesans presented the opportunity to paint the female nude in a realistic modern setting.

The blonde model for Manet's picture was the actress Henriette Hauser. Her well-known liaison with the Prince of Orange earned her the nickname "Citron," or lemon.

Nana, 1877
EDOUARD MANET, French, 1832–1883
Kunsthalle, Hamburg. Oil on canvas, 60¾ x 45¼ in.

Marriage

Let me not to the marriage of true minds
Admit impediments, love is not love
Which alters when it alteration finds,
Or bends with the remover to remove.
O no! it is an ever-fixed mark,
That looks on tempests and is never shaken;
It is the star to every wand'ring bark,
Whose worth's unknown, although his height be taken.
Love's not Time's fool, though rosy lips and cheeks
Within his bending sickle's compass come,
Love alters not with his brief hours and weeks,
But bears it out even to the edge of doom:
If this be error and upon me proved,
I never writ, nor no man ever loved.

WILLIAM SHAKESPEARE
Sonnet XVI

Royal Couples

The youthful couple portrayed in Sir Anthony Van Dyck's *Princess Mary Stuart and Prince William of Orange* regard the viewer with an endearing combination of childlike earnestness and princely pride. The occasion of the portrait was the couple's wedding, which took place on May 12, 1641. Princess Mary was the daughter of King Charles I of England and the great-granddaughter of Mary, Queen of Scots. Her husband was a prince of the House of Orange, leaders of the Dutch struggle for independence who later became the royal family of the Netherlands. The young couple lived during a turbulent period in English history. Civil war broke out in England the year after their marriage, and Charles I was beheaded in 1649, during the rise of Oliver Cromwell. After the Stuarts were restored to the throne in 1660, Princess Mary Stuart's brothers Charles II and James II reigned successively. In 1688, William of Orange, the son of the young couple in Van Dyck's painting, was invited to England, where he became King William III after the unpopular James II fled to France.

Van Dyck was the greatest of the pupils of the Flemish painter Peter Paul Rubens. After working in Antwerp and traveling in Italy he settled in England, and in 1632 became the court painter to Charles I and was knighted. The sumptuous brushwork and flattering elegance of his portrait style served as a model for two centuries of British aristocratic portraiture. The portrait of Princess Mary Stuart and Prince William of Orange was completed shortly before Van Dyck's death at the age of 42.

The painted relief from the lid of an Egyptian wooden and ivory chest represents the young pharoah Tutankhamun and his wife Ankhesenamun standing in a flower-garlanded arbor. Leaning on a staff, the king reaches forward to accept two bouquets of poppies, lotus, and papyrus from the youthful queen. Behind the figures, pillars ornamented with the same flowers support a vine-covered trellis over the couple's heads. The fresh beauty of the young couple and the simplicity of their gestures is contrasted with their richly ornamented surroundings. Tutankhamun was probably a son by a minor wife of the pharaoh Akhenaton, and succeeded to the throne at the age of about nine, upon the death of his father and his chosen successor. He was married to the daughter of Akhenaton and Queen Nefertiti, presumably to fortify the legitimacy of his succession. Most of his short reign (he was about 19 when he died) was devoted to reversing the radical innovations of Akhenaton, which had provoked opposition from his subjects. Tutankhamun reopened the temples of the gods that had been closed when Akhenaton proclaimed a monotheistic religion, and he abandoned the new capital that Akhenaton had built at Amarna, returning Egypt's seat of government to Thebes.

Princess Mary Stuart and Prince William of Orange, 1641

SIR ANTHONY VAN DYCK, Flemish, 1599–1641

Rijksmuseum, Amsterdam. Oil on canvas, 71 1/4 x 55 7/8 in.

Painted Wood and Ivory Chest

EGYPTIAN, New Kingdom, 18th Dynasty, Reign of Tutankhamun, 1334–1325 B.C.

Egyptian Museum, Cairo. Relief from the lid of a chest, carved wood veneered with ivory and painted.

❧ Betrothal

Dense with pattern and shimmering with light, Edouard Vuillard's *Interior* shows the workroom of his mother's dress and corset-making business on the Rue St. Honoré in Paris. Peering around the door of this female establishment is Vuillard's close friend, the artist Ker-Xavier Roussel. His shy but intent gaze rests on Vuillard's older sister Marie, whom he married in 1893, the year that this picture was painted. The couple's intense awareness of one another is subtly expressed in the alertness of their restrained poses, and in the slight tilt of Marie's head, which echoes Roussel's gesture. The energetic detachment of the woman folding cloth creates an amusing contrast with the quiet intensity of the engaged couple. Roussel had been a friend of Vuillard's since their school days and had introduced him to painting. The two friends formed part of a group of young French artists who called themselves the Nabis, after the Hebrew word for prophet. The work of the group tended to be rich in color and pattern and intimate in subject, although several of the artists painted theater décor and large decorative panels.

In Fra Filippo Lippi's *Portrait of a Man and a Woman at a Casement*, a couple exchanges steady but somewhat expressionless glances. The man's figure fills the entire height of the casement window, and his profile casts a shadow on the wall. His hands rest on the coat of arms of the Scolari family, an indication that this portrait was probably commissioned to celebrate an engagement or marriage. The couple represented may be Lorenzo Scolari and his wife Angiola di Bernardo Sapiti, who were married in 1436. The woman wears an elaborately embroidered headdress and a robe whose forms are rendered in strongly simplified geometric shapes. On her sleeve, lettering sewn in pearls reads "leal[tà]," or fidelity.

In 15th-century Tuscan portraits, women were represented in profile, which was thought to be the most flattering view. The painting reproduced here is the oldest surviving example of this type of Renaissance portraiture. It is also the earliest known Italian double portrait and one of the earliest European portraits showing a domestic interior. The landscape visible through the window is painted with a delicate observation of light and atmosphere and may have been inspired by Flemish painting.

Interior, 1893

EDOUARD VUILLARD, French, 1868–1940

Smith College Museum of Art, Northampton, Mass.
Oil on cardboard, 12½ x 14¹⁵⁄₁₆ in.

Portrait of a Man and a Woman at a Casement, c. 1440

FRA FILIPPO LIPPI, Italian, c. 1406–1469

The Metropolitan Museum of Art, New York, Gift of Henry G. Marquand, 1889, Marquand Collection. Tempera on wood, 25¼ x 16½ in.

FOLLOWING PAGES:DETAIL
Interior, 1893

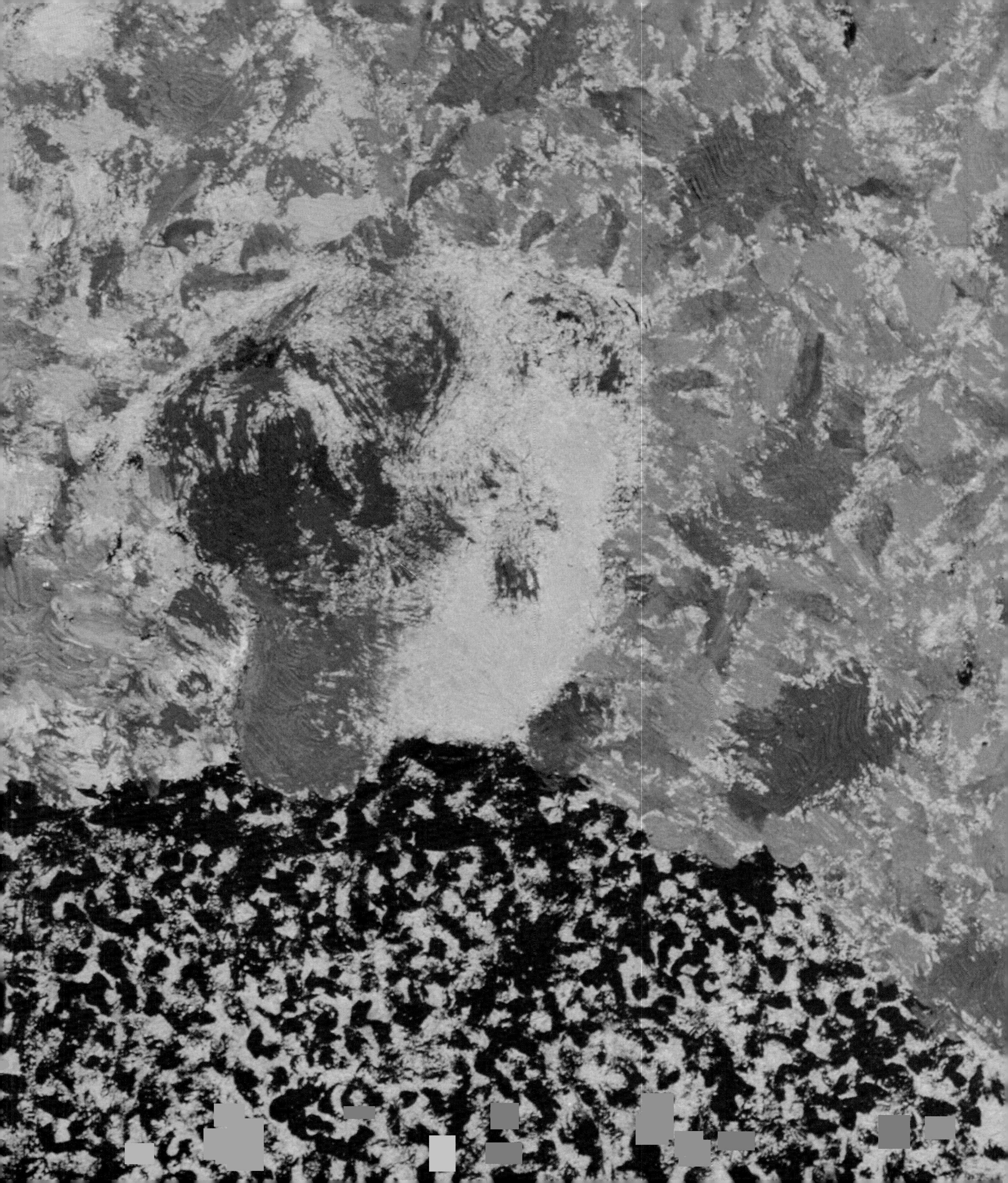

Bridal Couples

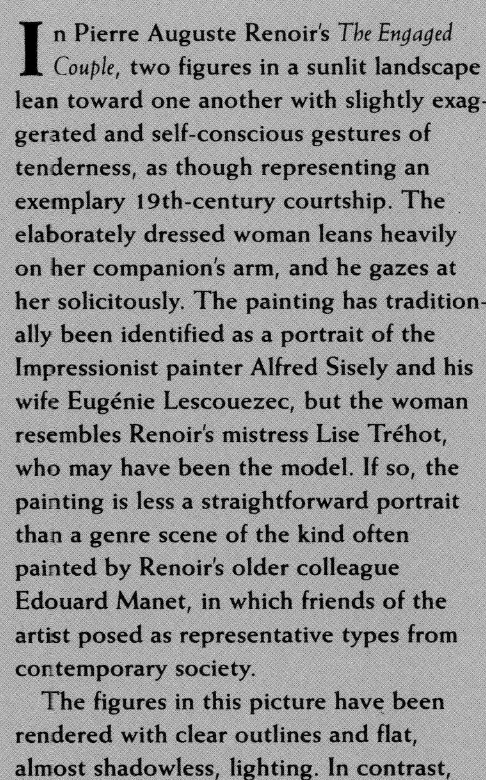

In Pierre Auguste Renoir's *The Engaged Couple*, two figures in a sunlit landscape lean toward one another with slightly exaggerated and self-conscious gestures of tenderness, as though representing an exemplary 19th-century courtship. The elaborately dressed woman leans heavily on her companion's arm, and he gazes at her solicitously. The painting has traditionally been identified as a portrait of the Impressionist painter Alfred Sisely and his wife Eugénie Lescouezec, but the woman resembles Renoir's mistress Lise Tréhot, who may have been the model. If so, the painting is less a straightforward portrait than a genre scene of the kind often painted by Renoir's older colleague Edouard Manet, in which friends of the artist posed as representative types from contemporary society.

The figures in this picture have been rendered with clear outlines and flat, almost shadowless, lighting. In contrast, the landscape has been loosely painted in dappled areas of light and shade. This difference in technique probably reflects the practice of adding figures painted in the studio to landscape backgrounds developed from outdoor sketches. This was the usual method of representing people in landscape settings until Renoir, Claude Monet, and their Impressionist colleagues began to paint outdoors in the 1860s, as a few landscape painters like Camille Corot had done before them. Completed when Renoir was still in his twenties and under the influence of older artists like Edouard Manet and Gustave Courbet, *The Engaged Couple* nonetheless foreshadows a duality of style that persisted throughout the artist's career. Alternating between the broken

The Engaged Couple, c. 1868
PIERRE AUGUSTE RENOIR, French, 1841–1919
Wallraf-Richartz Museum, Cologne. Oil on canvas, $42^{1}/_{4}$ x 30 in.

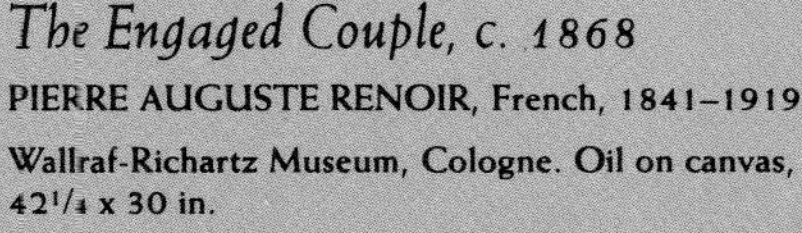

DETAIL
The Bridal Couple
REMBRANDT

brushwork and atmospheric color of Impressionism and the clear, solid draftsmanship of more traditional artists, Renoir struggled to unite two distinct methods of rendering form and space.

In Rembrandt's *The Bridal Couple*, the man reaches to embrace his wife, gazing at her lovingly as he places his hand gently on her breast. Staring into the distance, she touches his hand lightly with her fingertips. A golden light illuminates the upper bodies of the couple, drawing the viewer's attention to the sense of deep attachment expressed by their hands and faces.

The Bridal Couple is painted with the broad brushwork and rich reds and browns that are typical of Rembrandt's later works. The artist used thick layers of paint, called impasto, as a base, and then covered the underpainting with transparent glazes and small touches of color to give a brilliant sense of enveloping golden light to the scene. The luminous red of the bride's dress casts crimson reflections on the underside of the couple's linked arms.

The Bridal Couple, c. 1662
REMBRANDT HARMENSZ. VAN RIJN, Dutch, 1606–1669
Rijksmuseum, Amsterdam. Oil on canvas, 47³/₈ x 65 in.

❧ *The Wedding Ceremony*

In *The Marriage of Giovanni Arnolfini* by the great Flemish painter Jan van Eyck, the viewer becomes a witness to the exchange of marriage vows between the Italian merchant Giovanni Arnolfini and his bride Giovanna Cenami. Although the couple seems to be alone in their bridal chamber, two figures are reflected in the round mirror on the rear wall. An inscription above the mirror states that "Jan van Eyck was there," suggesting that one of the figures represents the artist.

Van Eyck was one of the Flemish painters who pioneered the development of oil painting in the early 15th century. Unlike the quick-drying tempera paints that had been used previously, the slow-drying, translucent quality of oil paints was well adapted to rendering light, atmosphere, and the physical textures of objects, and van Eyck used the new medium brilliantly to create a compellingly realistic vision of the world around him.

Imbedded in van Eyck's pictorial realism, however, is a symbolic language surviving from medieval art, and this picture contains subtle symbols that underscore the holiness of marriage. Although daylight illuminates the window, a lighted candle in the ornate brass chandelier represents the presence of God, and the couple have removed their shoes to indicate that they are standing on hallowed ground. The roundels in the mirror frame depict the Passion of Christ. The small dog in the foreground is emblematic of marital fidelity. Van Eyck has incorporated the world of the spirit into the world of physical reality in such a way that the painting is both a convincing document of an individual wedding and a testament to the sacramental nature of marriage itself.

DETAIL

The Marriage of Giovanni Arnolfini, 1434

JAN VAN EYCK, Flemish, c.1390–1441

The National Gallery, London. Oil on panel, 32¼ x 23½ in.

marc Chagall 938-39

Bride and Groom

In *The Wedding March*, Theodore Robinson has represented the marriage of his friend Theodore Butler in a fresh and informal Impressionist manner that shows the influence of Claude Monet, although his more concrete and careful draftsmanship reveals a typically American approach to the style. Robinson had met Monet through a friend and had visited the older artist at his home in Giverny, which he liked so well that he returned to live and work there. As other artists chanced upon the modest and attractive little village, word began to spread among the foreign artists studying in Paris, and Giverny found itself playing host to a growing colony of painters that included many Americans. Among them was Theodore Butler, whose bride, hidden by a windblown veil, was Monet's stepdaughter Suzanne Hoschedé.

In Marc Chagall's *The Bride and Groom of the Eiffel Tower*, the newlyweds are portrayed on the back of a large rooster, floating amid the visionary surroundings of a dream. The groom leans tenderly toward the bride, who stares before her with a gentle expression. An angel plays a violin below them and another appears upside down over the roofs of a village, holding a candelabra. Near the Eiffel Tower in the background, a third angel bears an offering of flowers, and a smiling goat merges with the forms of a string bass and a singer. In the background, the couple can be seen standing under their wedding canopy. The painting expresses a sense of memory, fantasy, and emotion, and in it, Chagall has created a lyrical, trancelike mood that is perfectly suited to the depiction of a wedding day.

The Wedding March, 1892

THEODORE ROBINSON, American, 1852-1896

Terra Museum of American Art, Chicago, Daniel J. Terra Collection. Oil on canvas, 22 x 26 in.

The Bride and Groom of the Eiffel Tower, 1938–1939

MARC CHAGALL, Russian, 1887–1985

Musée National d'Art Moderne, Paris. Oil on canvas, $59^{1}/_{4}$ x $57^{1}/_{8}$ in.

The scene painted on the Greek marriage vase illustrated here represents the arrival of a newlywed bride and groom at their house. Wrapped in a cloak that is drawn up over her head, the bride stands hesitantly on the threshold, supported by an attendant. The groom guides her toward her new home, holding her by the wrist in a ritual gesture. With lowered heads, the couple exchange intimate and tender glances. The scene continues around the vase. Behind the bride's attendant, a procession carries wedding gifts, and to the right of the groom, a flute player and a torchbearer wait inside the house to welcome the husband and wife.

This type of wedding vase is called a *loutrophoros*. More elongated and slender in shape than the common amphora used for storing wine or oil, the *loutrophoros* was used to carry water for the baths that formed part of both marriage and funeral rituals. The ceremony represented on the side of the *loutrophoros* indicates its intended function.

Ankhesenamun Assisting at the Toilet of Tutankhamun is a relief from a throne found in the tomb of the young pharaoh. The scene was carved on the wooden panel of the throne's back, then covered in sheet gold and ornamented with silver, faience, colored glass, and translucent stones. The royal couple is shown in a pavilion. Columns ornamented with flowers support a roof with a frieze of cobras and sun disks. The pharaoh Tutankhamun, seated on a chair with blue lion's-paw feet, is attended by his wife Ankhesenamun, who is anointing him with perfume from a vial that she holds in her left hand. Both figures wear elaborate crowns and broad jeweled collars. A similar collar rests on a stand behind the queen. Although this may be a scene from Tutankhamun's coronation, the intimacy and casualness of the couple's gestures are surprising on a piece of state furniture. The informality of this scene echoes the style of Tutankhamun's predecessor, the pharaoh Akhenaton, who imposed on Egypt the monotheistic worship of the sun god Aton and who encouraged the development of a new naturalistic style in art. Aton's golden disk shines down on the royal couple with rays that terminate in human hands.

Ankhesenamun Assisting at the Toilet of Tutankhamun

EGYPTIAN, New Kingdom, 18th Dynasty, Reign of Tutankhamun, c. 1334–1325 B.C.

Egyptian Museum, Cairo. Relief from the back of a throne. Carved wood covered with sheer gold inlaid with colored glass, faience, and translucent stone painted at the back.

Newlyweds Arrive at their House, from a loutrophoros (marriage vase), *c. 460 B.C.*

SABOUROFF PAINTER, Greek

National Museum, Copenhagen, Inv. no. 9080. Pottery, height 26 in.

❧ *Husband and Wife*

In the Egyptian sculpture illustrated here, the Old Kingdom pharaoh Mycerinus and his queen stand side by side. The queen embraces her husband and places a hand on his arm, conveying a sense of affection and pride. The monarch and his wife are represented in their prime, and their gracefully proportioned bodies give the viewer a glimpse into Egyptian ideals of male and female beauty. His torso bare, Mycerinus wears a pharaonic headdress, false beard, and a linen kilt, and his wife wears a clinging robe that reveals the swelling contours of her body. Broad-shouldered and slim-hipped, the figures stand with their left feet forward, but their bodies give no sense of motion.

Like most Egyptian sculpture, this piece is actually a high relief, for the figures are attached to a background slab. Sculptures like this one were chiseled from a single block with stone hammers and then ground and polished with abrasives. This piece came from Giza, where the tomb of Mycerinus is one of the three most famous Egyptian pyramids. It stands beside the pyramid of Mycerinus' father Chephren, guarded by the sphinx, and that of his grandfather, known as the Great Pyramid of Cheops.

In *Rubens and His Wife, Isabella, in the Honeysuckle Arbor*, the Flemish artist Peter Paul Rubens commemorated his marriage in 1609 to the 17-year-old Isabella Brant, the daughter of a prominent Antwerp lawyer and humanist. Earlier in the same year, Rubens' brother Phillip had married Isabella's aunt. Hand in hand, the elaborately dressed couple gaze toward the spectator with a mixture of solemnity and pride. The 32-year-old Rubens sits in a pose of self-conscious casualness, with his legs crossed and his hand resting on the gilded hilt of a sword. Isabella's face is framed between her starched lace ruff and the broad brim of her high-crowned straw hat.

Rubens had returned to Antwerp the previous year from Italy, where he had spent eight years studying ancient sculpture and the work of Renaissance masters and absorbing the Italian artistic tradition. He had recently been appointed as the court painter to the Spanish regent and had established a studio in Antwerp to carry out royal commissions. Rubens had evidently been introduced to diplomacy as a career by members of the Brant family living in Holland, and he was valued at court both as a painter and as a diplomatic advisor and emissary.

Mycerinus and His Queen, c. 2470 B.C.
EGYPTIAN, Old Kingdom, 4th Dynasty
Museum of Fine Arts, Boston, Harvard MFA Expedition. Slate, height 54½ in.

Rubens and His Wife, Isabella, in the Honeysuckle Arbor, 1609–1610
PETER PAUL RUBENS, Flemish, 1577–1640
Alte Pinakothek, Munich. Oil on canvas, 69½ x 53¼ in.

Thomas Gainsborough's *Mr. and Mrs. Andrews* portrays the young couple on the grounds of their Sudbury estate, in Suffolk, looking very much the British squire and his lady. Robert Andrews adopts a pose of studied nonchalance, standing cross-legged and leaning on the arm of the garden bench, with his hand in his pocket and his rifle tucked casually under his arm. His round and rather solemn face is framed by a tricorne hat worn at a jaunty angle. His wife sits primly on the bench, her hands in her lap and her small feet neatly crossed at the ankles. She wears a beautifully rendered blue silk dress and a lace cap topped by a beribboned hat. Her expression, though piquant, is difficult to interpret. The couple's position at the side of the painting emphasizes the importance of their setting. Beyond them extends a landscape painted with extraordinary freshness and charm. Large trees, stacked grain, and sheep in fenced pastures all attest to the continuing and careful husbandry of the estate. Above the rolling hills in the distance, a luminous and cloud-filled sky gives the impression of the shifting sunlight and shadow of an overcast day.

Gainsborough was still in his early twenties when he completed his portrait of Mr. and Mrs. Andrews, who had been married a year or two previously. At the time of the commission, the artist had recently returned to his native Sudbury after completing his training in London. There, he had studied the paintings of the French artist Antoine Watteau, whose graceful and delicately proportioned figures influenced his early work. Gainsborough also studied the work of 17th-century Dutch landscape artists, and in particular, the paintings of Jacob van Ruisdael, whose atmospheric, cloud-filled skies inspired his treatment of the landscape in the Andrews portrait. After working in Sudbury for about nine years, Gainsborough moved to the town of Bath, where he soon attracted the attention of the fashionable world.

Mr. and Mrs. Andrews, c. 1748–1750
THOMAS GAINSBOROUGH, British, 1727–1788
The National Gallery, London. Oil on canvas, 27⅞ x 47 in.

Relaxed Intimacy

Charles Willson Peale's *Benjamin and Eleanor Ridgely Laming* portrays an attractive middle-aged couple in an informal and affectionate pose. Leaning toward his wife, Benjamin Laming gazes at her fondly, while she looks directly ahead of her with a slightly abstracted expression. Her hand, holding a sprig of berries, is laid casually on his arm. A corsage of flowers ornaments her dress and three peaches and a spray of leaves rest in her lap. In American 18th-century portraiture, women were often associated with fruit and flowers, which were probably symbolic of fertility. Benjamin Laming holds a telescope. Behind him, at the left edge of the painting, is a parrot with a blue face and red wing markings. In contrast to Gainsborough's portrait of Mr. and Mrs. Andrews (page 114–115), Peale's couple fills the entire foreground of the painting and eclipses the landscape behind them.

In Edouard Manet's *Argenteuil*, a couple sits with an air of relaxed intimacy at the edge of a yacht basin. Holding his companion's parasol, the man leans forward as though he is trying to attract her attention. She stares somewhat expressionlessly ahead of her, slumping slightly and holding a bunch of daisies and poppies in her lap. The man's straw hat, jersey, and espadrilles suit the informality of a holiday gathering place, while the woman's slightly garish dress and fanciful hat identify her as a member of the lower middle class. The resort town of Argenteuil was known as a place where boatmen of all classes associated with women of questionable morals, and Manet's contemporaries debated the nature of the relationship between the couple when this painting was shown in the Paris Salon of 1875. Although the picture's setting was associated with casual encounters, the poses of the figures suggest relaxed and unconscious intimacy.

Manet seems to have painted outdoors for the first time during the summer of 1874, encouraged by the *plein-air* pictures of his younger colleagues Claude Monet and Pierre Auguste Renoir. The painting reproduced here is one of the most impressionistic of Manet's works. Filled with a shimmering light, it is nonetheless organized by means of a very orderly composition of verticals and horizontals. The upright figure of the woman is echoed by the vertical masts and smokestacks behind her, while the diagonal lines of the man's cross-legged figure are repeated in the rigging of the boat behind him. The two figures are separated from the factories and houses of Argenteuil by water of an astonishingly intense blue.

Benjamin and Eleanor Ridgely Laming, 1788
CHARLES WILLSON PEALE, American, 1741–1827
National Gallery of Art, Washington, D.C. Oil on canvas, 42 x 60¼ in.

Argenteuil, 1874
EDOUARD MANET, French, 1832–1883
Musée des Beaux Arts, Tournai. Oil on canvas, 59 3/4 x 45¼ in.

Manet 1874

A Reunited Couple

The two paintings reproduced here represent incidents from the story of Ulysses, the hero of Homer's *Odyssey*, and his wife Penelope. At the outset of the tale, Ulysses, noted for his intelligence and cunning, was returning to Ithaca after ten years of fighting in the Trojan War. However, his ship was wrecked during a storm raised by the angry goddess Athena, and he was detained on the island of the enchantress Circe through the wrath of the sea god Poseidon, whose son Polyphemus had been blinded by Ulysses. Thus began a series of adventures that prevented Ulysses' return home for another decade. During this time, the beautiful Penelope was besieged by suitors hoping to marry her and usurp Ulysses' throne. Refusing to choose among them until she had finished weaving a shroud for her father-in-law, she delayed matters by unraveling each day's labor at night until a maidservant betrayed her and she was forced to finish.

Pinturicchio's *Scenes from the Odyssey* depicts Penelope seated at her loom as her son Telemachus returns from searching for his father. Ulysses, disguised as a beggar, enters the room to test the fidelity of his wife, approving of her plan to accept whichever suitor could string and shoot Ulysses' bow. During the contest, the supposed beggar revealed his identity by succeeding after the others had failed. After a battle in which the suitors were killed, peace was returned to the kingdom. In this fresco, painted for a palace in Siena, Pinturicchio has created a delightful view of an upper-class Renaissance home and filled the scene with amusing details such as the cat in the foreground playing with a ball of yarn.

In contrast to the sprightly narrative contained in Pinturicchio's painting, Francesco Primaticcio's *Ulysses and Penelope* offers an intimate and moving view of the reunited couple. As Penelope solemnly counts the time of his absence on her fingers, Ulysses cradles her chin in his hand and gazes at her with a searching and tender expression. This painting is based on a fresco, now lost, that Primaticcio painted in the royal palace of the French king Francis I at Fontainebleau.

Scenes from the Odyssey, c. 1509
BERNARDINO DI BETTO, CALLED PINTURICCHIO, Italian, c. 1454–1513
The National Gallery, London. Fresco, transferred to canvas, 49½ x 59¾ in.

Ulysses and Penelope, c. 1560
FRANCESCO PRIMATICCIO, Italian, 1504–1570
Toledo Museum of Art, Ohio. Oil on canvas, 44 x 48 in.

FOLLOWING PAGES: DETAIL
Scenes from the Odyssey

Industry and Idleness

Every couple forms a unique culture of its own, as its partners develop habits, rituals, private jokes or allusions, and a shared past. The two paintings reproduced here show how drastically these cultures may vary.

James and Sarah Tuttle, by the American folk artist Joseph H. Davis, represents a pair of people who are clearly beyond reproach. Dressed in black, they are seated on either side of a marbleized table that holds a top hat and a bowl of fruit. The man points to a verse in the open Bible as his wife holds a small red prayer book. Surrounded by a garland of leaves, a framed print representing a lumber mill hangs on the wall, and a small cat sits underneath the table. The symmetrical organization of the figures in this picture, their flat shapes, and the emphatic patterns of areas such as the table and the rug are all hallmarks of a self-trained folk artist. The symmetry of this picture and its careful details as well as the upright formality of the couple's rigid poses express an earnest desire for order and correctness on the part of artist and sitters alike.

Unlike the Davis picture, which is a portrait of those hoping to be remembered at their best, Jan Steen's *The Sleeping Couple* is a moralizing genre painting intended to warn its audience about the perils of idleness and drunkeness. With relish, Steen has portrayed a man and a woman who have accepted and reinforced one another's faults and who have lost control of their own behavior. Near a garden wall with a grape arbor and a hanging flask, Steen's figures sleep at a table strewn with nutshells, a book, and a bottle. Behind them, presenting an ironic commentary on their state, a urinating statue of a cupid ornaments a fountain.

A prolific artist, Steen was the foremost painter of low-life Dutch genre pictures in the latter 17th century. His scenes of raucousness and debauchery are painted with such gusto and humor that it is easy for the modern viewer to forget that they were intended to instruct as well as to amuse.

The Sleeping Couple

JAN STEEN, Dutch, 1625/6–1679

Corporation of London, Harold Samuel Collection. Oil on copper, 7 x 9 in.

James and Sarah Tuttle, 1836

JOSEPH H. DAVIS, American, active 1830s

The New-York Historical Society. Watercolor on paper, 9 1/2 x 14 1/2 in.

Moments of Boredom

Each of the two paintings reproduced here takes as its subject the moments of isolation, boredom, or self-absorption that can occur in a marriage, but their approaches to the topic could hardly be more dissimilar. Edward Hopper's *Room in New York* conveys a quiet sense of the loneliness that is part of the human condition and that is present as a frequent undercurrent in the artist's work. William Hogarth's picture bristles with narrative detail and forms a part of the artist's fierce indictment of the social failures that he saw surrounding him in 18th-century London.

Hogarth's *Marriage à la Mode: Morning* (pages 125–127) is the second in a series of six pictures portraying the disastrous course of an arranged marriage between the dissolute heir of a noble family and the rich but uncultivated young woman whose fortune they are rapidly squandering. Evidence of the couple's self-indulgence and irresponsibility abounds in the painting and foretells the final catastrophe—the husband's death in a duel with his wife's lover and his wife's subsequent suicide. Lord Squanderfield has flung himself into a chair, exhausted after an arduous night on the town. His broken sword lies at his feet, and a woman's lace cap dangles from his pocket. His wife stretches in an inelegant but provocative manner. Hoyle's book on whist lies at her feet, and in the background, a servant tidies up the aftermath of her card party as candles gutter in the chandelier. The sheet music near the overturned chair suggests that she has had a music lesson, perhaps hastily interrupted on her husband's return. The two violins have evidently remained in their closed cases during the lesson. The couple's steward is departing in despair, having failed to

Room in New York. 1932

EDWARD HOPPER, American, 1882–1967

F. M. Hall Collection, Sheldon Memorial Art Gallery, University of Nebraska, Lincoln. Oil on canvas, 29 x 36 in.

interest his master and mistress in the sheaf of unpaid bills that he has brought with him.

In contrast to Hogarth's dramatic narrative, Hopper presents the viewer with his quiet refusal to tell a story. Instead, in *Room in New York*, the viewer gazes through a window like a voyeur at a brilliantly illuminated scene of banal isolation. As the husband concentrates on his paper, his wife idly turns to finger the keys of the piano, breaking the silence that fills the modest room. The bright light accentuates the painting's crisp contrasts of black and white and the reddish accents of the chair, dress, and lampshade. The faces of the husband and wife are in shadow, reinforcing the sense of this scene as a private moment in which intimacy and loneliness are intertwined.

Marriage à la Mode: Morning, 1743

WILLIAM HOGARTH, British, 1697–1764

The National Gallery, London. Oil on canvas, 27 1/2 x 35 3/4 in.

Friendly Gestures

These two pictures portray friendly and slightly flirtatious behavior on the part of the couples represented. William Hogarth's portrait of his friend David Garrick shows the famous actor seated at his desk, writing the prologue for one of his comedies. Behind him, his wife, Eva Mary Veigel, reaches playfully for his quill pen. A well-known dancer, she performed under the stage name of Mademoiselle Violette. The lighthearted quality of the picture is accentuated by Garrick's theatrical pose and the drooping spray of flowers in his buttonhole, and by the elaborate lace flounces on his wife's dress. In spite of their friendship, Garrick and Hogarth apparently quarreled at the final sitting for the painting, and Hogarth crossed out the eyes of the actor's portrait, which were later repainted. The portrait remained in Hogarth's studio at his death and was given to Garrick by the artist's widow.

Edouard Manet's *In the Conservatory* is a portrait of the artist's friends M. and Mme. Jules Guillemet, owners of a fashionable dress shop on the Rue St. Honoré in Paris. Evidently caught during a pause in the conversation, Mme. Guillemet, an American known for her beauty and Parisian stylishness, stares abstractedly before her. Her husband, whose strong resemblance to Manet was noted by their friends, leans attentively forward, pointing with his forefinger toward his wife's outstretched hand. His slightly flirtatious gesture is underlined by Mme. Guillemet's furled parasol below the couple's hands. In spite of the Guillemets' prominent wedding rings, the conservatory setting of their conversation lends a slightly ambiguous tone to the picture. Conservatories, fashionable additions to the houses of the newly rich, offered privacy for couples, and Emile Zola had used one as the setting for a scene of adulterous betrayal in a novel published eight years earlier. The association would have been familiar to Parisians who saw Manet's picture in the Salon of 1879, and a contemporary caricature of the painting was captioned, "An innocent young person cornered in the conservatory by an infamous seducer."

In the Conservatory, 1879
EDOUARD MANET, French, 1832–1883
Nationalgalerie, Staatliche Museen Preussischer Kulturbesitz, Berlin. Oil on canvas, 45 1/4 x 59 in.

David Garrick and His Wife, 1747
WILLIAM HOGARTH, British, 1697–1764
Royal Collection, Windsor. Oil on canvas, 37 x 28 1/4 in.

Old Married Couples

Perhaps in response to the tedium of sitting for their portraits, Raphael Soyer's mother and father have struck poses of emphatic, almost theatrical, resignation. Their gestures, affectionately described in *The Artist's Parents*, seem to express a lifetime of well-earned weariness. Although each partner stares vacantly into some private reverie, the similar slump of their down-to-earth poses and their identical gazes, with raised eyebrows and lowered eyelids, convey the unconscious unity of a man and woman who have grown together through experience. The smallness of their figures is evident from the height of the table. Soyer has illuminated his mother's face with a strong light that emphasizes the modeling of her features. In contrast, her hands have been rendered with a few sketchy lines.

Like his brothers Israel and Moses, Raphael Soyer belonged to a group of New York painters who rejected the modernist styles such as cubism that were arriving from Europe around the time of the First World War. Instead, this group produced modest and appealing figure paintings describing the life of New York's working class.

By contrast, Paul Klee, a member of the Bauhaus, was very much a modern artist, although his work owes its origins to no specific movement. Combining abstraction and primitivism, Klee's work is a unique blend of formal inventiveness and playful wit. The artist's *Old Married Couple* (pages 132–133) offers a gently humorous view of a husband and wife who have literally grown together over time. The top of the man's head, his wife's chin, and her hairdo have been described by the unbroken

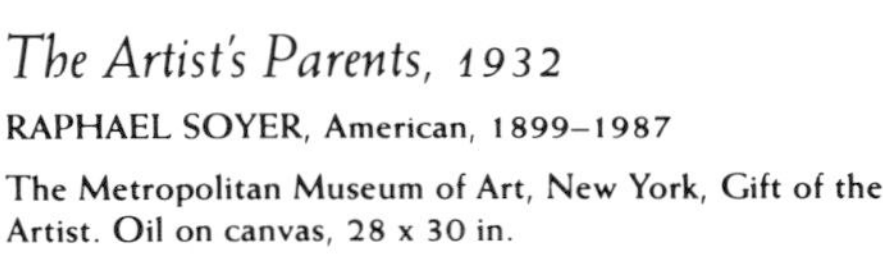

The Artist's Parents, 1932

RAPHAEL SOYER, American, 1899–1987

The Metropolitan Museum of Art, New York, Gift of the Artist. Oil on canvas, 28 x 30 in.

curves of a long arabesque that moves across the canvas like a melodic line in a piece of music. The noses and mouths of the man and woman, though differently formed, are rearrangements of the same elements: a curved line, two dots, and a crescent shape. In spite of the painting's considerable degree of abstraction, Klee has given the viewer an amusingly clear idea of the differing roles played by each member of this couple. The man, with closed eyes, seems quietly self-absorbed as his wife regards him with bright-eyed, twittering attention.

FOLLOWING PAGES:

Old Married Couple, 1931

PAUL KLEE, Swiss, 1879–1940

Norton Gallery, West Palm Beach, Florida. Tempera on burlap, 13 x 18¾ in.

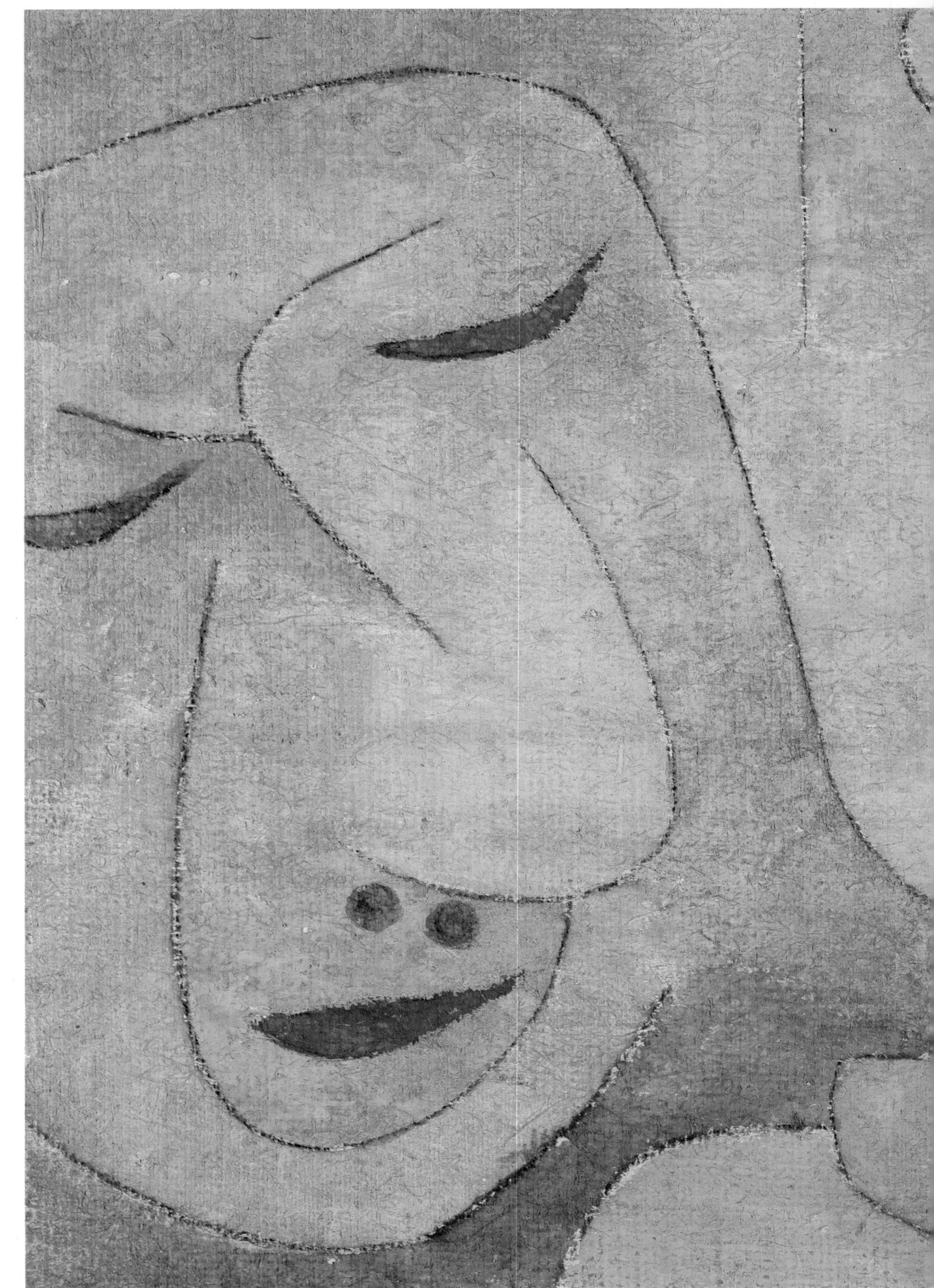

Parting & Loss

So, we'll go no more a-roving
So late into the night,
Though the heart be still as loving,
And the moon be still as bright.

For the sword outwears its sheath,
And the soul wears out the breast,
And the heart must pause to breathe,
And love itself have rest.

Though the night was made for loving,
And the day returns too soon,
Yet we'll go no more a-roving
By the light of the moon.

LORD BYRON

☙ *Reluctant Parting*

In Gerard ter Borch's *Unwelcome News*, a soldier sits before a curtained bed in a shadowy interior, with his arm around a wistful girl. In his hand, he holds the orders recalling him to duty. The blond officer who has come with the orders is bedecked with military regalia. He wears a sword, spurs, and, slung over his shoulder, a trumpet with a richly embroidered green banner. The sorrowful expressions of the parting couple are delicately and poignantly rendered.

Ter Borch began his career as a painter of barrack and guardroom scenes, often representing soldiers in sentimental situations. Later, he specialized in elegant depictions of upper-class people engaged in reading, letter writing, conversation, music making, and flirtation. Ter Borch's paintings are distinguished by the gracefulness of his slender figures and by the artist's brilliant rendering of silk and satin. In the painting reproduced here, the banner and the girl's skirt demonstrate his skill at depicting the sparkle of light on rich fabric.

The Unwelcome Message, 1653

GERARD TER BORCH, Dutch, 1617–1681

Mauritshuis, The Hague. Oil on panel, 26 x 23 1/4 in.

☙ Difficult Confrontations

Henri Matisse's *Conversation* depicts the artist and his wife Amélie facing one another in a room with walls of an intense blue. Matisse stands with his hands in his pockets, wearing striped pajamas that bear some resemblance to a prisoner's uniform, while Amélie Matisse is seated, wearing a black bathrobe that lends her the air of a presiding judge. In fact, Matisse based the composition of this painting on an ancient Assyrian relief in the Louvre depicting the king Hammurabi standing reverently before the seated god Shamash as he dictates the law. Locked in a confrontation of wills, the artist and his wife stare at one another in stony silence, indicating tensions in the marriage that eventually led to the Matisses' separation in 1919.

A garden bursts into springtime bloom outside the window, which is ornamented with symmetrical iron scrollwork spelling out the word "non." The vibrant blue of the bare room underscores the painting's mood of isolation and silence.

Edgar Degas' *Interior* (pages 142–143) is one of the artist's masterpieces, and yet the scene that it represents remains mysterious, in spite of its extraordinary atmosphere of tension and crisis. This ambiguity of meaning seems to have been quite deliberate on the artist's part. What is apparent is that a woman crouches miserably on a chair in a lamplit room, her chemise pulled down over one shoulder. A man leans against the door with a proprietary and somewhat brutal air, his hands in his pockets and his legs spread apart. The lamp shines brightly on the pink interior of an empty jewel box, and a woman's corset and a man's garments are strewn across the bed and floor.

The source for this tense and sinister scene may have been Emile Zola's novel *Thérèse Raquin*, which had caused a scandal at the time of its publication in 1867. Zola was a friend of Manet and Cézanne, and his writings were read with interest by artists in Degas' circle. In the book, the heroine and her lover marry after murdering her first husband. Zola described the couple's wedding night in a scene similar to the one that Degas depicted. Ill at ease together in a lamplit room, the couple discovers that a growing sense of guilt has destroyed their love for one another.

Conversation, 1909
HENRI MATISSE, French, 1869–1954
Hermitage, Leningrad. Oil on canvas, 69 3/4 x 85 1/2 in.

FOLLOWING PAGES
Interior, 1868–1869
EDGAR DEGAS, French, 1834–1917
Philadelphia Museum of Art, Henry P. McIlhenny Collection. Oil on canvas, 32 x 45 in.

Fickleness and Change

William Sidney Mount's *Sportsman's Last Visit* depicts a moment of painful discovery on the part of the rough-and-ready outdoorsman who has entered this modest rural room. Undoubtedly prepared to regale his sweetheart with long and tedious tales of his hunting triumphs, he has found himself replaced by a suave, well-dressed suitor who leans forward to engage her in conversation. She coyly tilts her head to stare at a length of ribbon in her lap. Her gesture is clear, and her elegant dress leaves little doubt about which suitor she prefers.

Mount painted this picture at a time when American artists were becoming interested in depicting scenes of daily life and describing the characteristics of their neighbors. Often during this period, as artists and writers sought to define a national identity, they contrasted rugged and rural "American" types with more genteel and sophisticated urban characters. Mount painted this picture in his twenties. His later works were simpler and more monumental in style, and were more likely to represent a moment in time than to tell a story.

In *The Neglected Lady*, by an anonymous Indian artist, a despondent woman is seated on a carpet in the moonlit evening. She is clearly waiting in vain for her absent lover as she leans against a large cushion, attended by two companions. One of them holds an elegant fly whisk, and the other, with an expression of concern, seems to be offering advice. From a window in the background, a man wearing a crown watches them. He has light blue skin, a complexion recalling that of the Hindu god Krishna, famous for his romantic exploits with mortals and his love of the human woman Radha.

The term Kangra describes a style of painting that flourished during the late 18th and early 19th century in northern India, in the small Rajput courts of the Himalayan foothills. Kangra art contained elements drawn from two distinct traditions of Indian art. One was the flat, brightly colored, stylized, and symbolic art of the Hindu tradition, to which the rulers of the courts belonged. The other was the Mughal style, which was practiced by some of the artists who moved to the courts after the dissolution of the Mughal empire. This tradition had its origins in Persian and Islamic art and was influenced by European painting. It was more naturalistic and used effects of atmosphere and shading. Kangra artists took particular pleasure in representing elegant court ladies and in depicting Krishna's romantic adventures.

The Sportsman's Last Visit, 1835
WILLIAM SIDNEY MOUNT, American, 1807–1868
The Museums at Stony Brook, Stony Brook, N.Y. Gift of Mr. and Mrs. Ward Melville, 1958. Oil on canvas, 21 1/2 x 17 1/2 in.

The Neglected Lady, c. 1850
INDIAN, Kangra, 19th century
Victoria and Albert Museum, London. Gouache on paper, 11 3/8 x 7 5/8 in.

Parting in Anger

The angry young man in Roy Lichtenstein's *Forget It! Forget Me!* stalks away from a girl behind him, who stares at him with an anguished expression. The closed, impassive quality of the man's face, seen in a dramatic closeup, contrasts with the girl's open mouth and knitted brows. His greatly enlarged figure is cut in half by the picture's edge, as though he were walking toward a camera.

Lichtenstein has depicted this emotional moment in the style of a comic book, emphasizing the origin of the image in inexpensive commercial printing processes. In an ironic, deadpan manner, he contrasts the dramatic exaggeration of the scene with the banality of its source. A founder of American Pop art, Lichtenstein has experimented in many ways with Benday dots and other elements of commercial illustration, combining them with a wide variety of artistic sources, including the work of Matisse, Léger, and many other earlier 20th-century painters.

In Dirk Hals' *Woman Tearing up a Letter*, the end of another affair appears to be at hand. Illuminated by a shaft of light falling through the large window, a young woman with a pained expression shreds the letter that has caused her disappointment. Correspondence was a common theme in 17th-century Dutch painting, and most of the letter writing was apparently devoted to love. In countless pictures, letters were written laboriously in parlors and guardrooms, delivered by servants, and read with varying emotions. Letter writing became fashionable in Holland during the middle of the century, and manuals were published containing graceful letters for all occasions to be used by those who lacked writing ability or inspiration.

Dirk Hals was the younger brother of the more famous painter Frans Hals, who specialized in portraiture. The reactions of his letter readers were depicted in a much more direct and obvious manner than was the case in the work of other genre painters such as Gerard ter Borch and Jan Vermeer.

Forget It! Forget Me!, 1962

ROY LICHTENSTEIN, American, 1923–

Rose Art Museum, Brandeis University, Waltham, Mass., Gerritz-Mnuchin Purchase Fund. Acrylic and oil on canvas, 81 3/8 x 69 1/2 in.

Woman Tearing up a Letter, 1631

DIRCK HALS, Dutch, 1591–1656

Landesmuseum, Mainz. Oil on panel, 17 3/4 x 21 7/8 in.

ꕤ *Farewell Scenes*

Titian's vision of a pastoral landscape inhabited by gods and mortals inspired painters for several centuries. His *Venus and Adonis* represents a scene of parting lovers from a story told by the Roman poet Ovid. In this tragic tale, the goddess Venus fell in love with the mortal Adonis. Titian's painting shows her in the act of trying to restrain him from leaving on a boar hunt. With her divine foresight, she knows that he will be killed, but she is powerless to restrain the impulsive young huntsman.

Titian's arrangement of these two figures represents an extraordinary tour de force of composition. From head to foot, Venus and Adonis are each twisted into a 180-degree turn, and their limbs combine to form a pinwheel shape. The dynamic, rotary motion of their flailing arms and legs expresses the beseeching grief of the goddess and the heedless impatience of the departing mortal. Venus was borrowed from a frequently copied figure on an ancient relief, and her beautifully painted back and head demonstrate the brilliant technique of this great Venetian painter.

In *Cephalus and Aurora*, Nicolas Poussin also depicts a scene from a story recounted by Ovid, in which Aurora, the goddess of the dawn, fell in love with the mortal Cephalus. In the painting, Cephalus turns away from Aurora when a cupid shows him a picture of his wife Procris. Poussin has created a dream-like vision of the classical world, in which divinities and natural forces mingle and communicate with humans. The figures of the clinging goddess and the reluctant Cephalus are as

Venus and Adonis, c. 1560

TIZIANO VECELLIO, CALLED TITIAN, Italian, 1487-1576

National Gallery of Art, Washington, D.C., Widener Collection. Oil on canvas, 42 x 53½ in.

DETAIL

Cephalus and Aurora

NICOLAS POUSSIN

expressively choreographed as a pair of dancers, and the poetic quality of this pagan landscape is reinforced by the sleeping river god in the foreground and the magnificent winged horse Pegasus standing under the trees. In the distance, a reclining goddess watches the sun god Apollo drive his chariot through the sky, starting a new day.

Poussin was the most important French painter of the 17th century. He spent most of his career working in Rome, where he pursued his lifelong fascination with classical antiquity. The picture reproduced here is one of the artist's early works and reflects his admiration for the paintings of Titian.

Cephalus and Aurora, c. 1630
NICOLAS POUSSIN, French, 1594–1665
The National Gallery, London. Oil on canvas, 38 x 51 in.

Heartbreak

Jan Steen's *The Lovesick Maiden* is one of at least 18 pictures in which the Dutch artist portrayed the visits of doctors to young women who were suffering the pains of romantic melancholy or the more embarrassing affliction of unexpected pregnancy. These doctors, often represented as quacks wearing old-fashioned garments, applied a variety of folk techniques to diagnose the problem. In the painting reproduced here, a distraught young woman in a tight red bodice holds her hand to her forehead as a doctor feels her wrist to see if a racing pulse indicates the presence of her lover. A ribbon from the girl's garment smolders in a brazier so that the quack doctor can decide from the smell of the smoke whether or not she is pregnant. An older woman bends solicitously toward the doctor to hear his verdict on the case. A statue of a cupid over the doorway and the pair of mating dogs in the background emphasize the erotic nature of the girl's complaint.

In contrast to Steen's jovial humor, Francis Danby's *Disappointed Love* (pages 154–155) presents a stark and poignant image of heartbreak. A young woman in a white dress sits at the edge of a stream with her head buried in her lap, in an attitude of intense despair. She has flung off her bonnet and shawl, which lie beside her, along with a miniature portrait of a young man and an open wallet containing a letter. Torn scraps of paper float along the surface of the stream.

Danby has used several techniques to reinforce the drama of his narrative. The girl's white dress, associated with innocence, contrasts with the darkness of her surroundings. The gloomy trees and the overgrown plants lend a sinister atmosphere to the painting and suggest the possibility of death. The broad-leaved plants in the foreground, choked with ivy and brambles, have been painted with a direct, almost naive intensity of observation.

The Lovesick Maiden, c 1660s

JAN STEEN, Dutch, 1625/6–1679

The Metropolitan Museum of Art, New York, Bequest of Helen Swift Neilson, 1945, Oil on canvas, 34 x 39 in.

FOLLOWING PAGES

Disappointed Love, exhibited 1821

FRANCIS DANBY, Irish, 1793–1861

Victoria and Albert Museum, London. Oil on wood. 24 3/4 x 32 in.

I STEEN

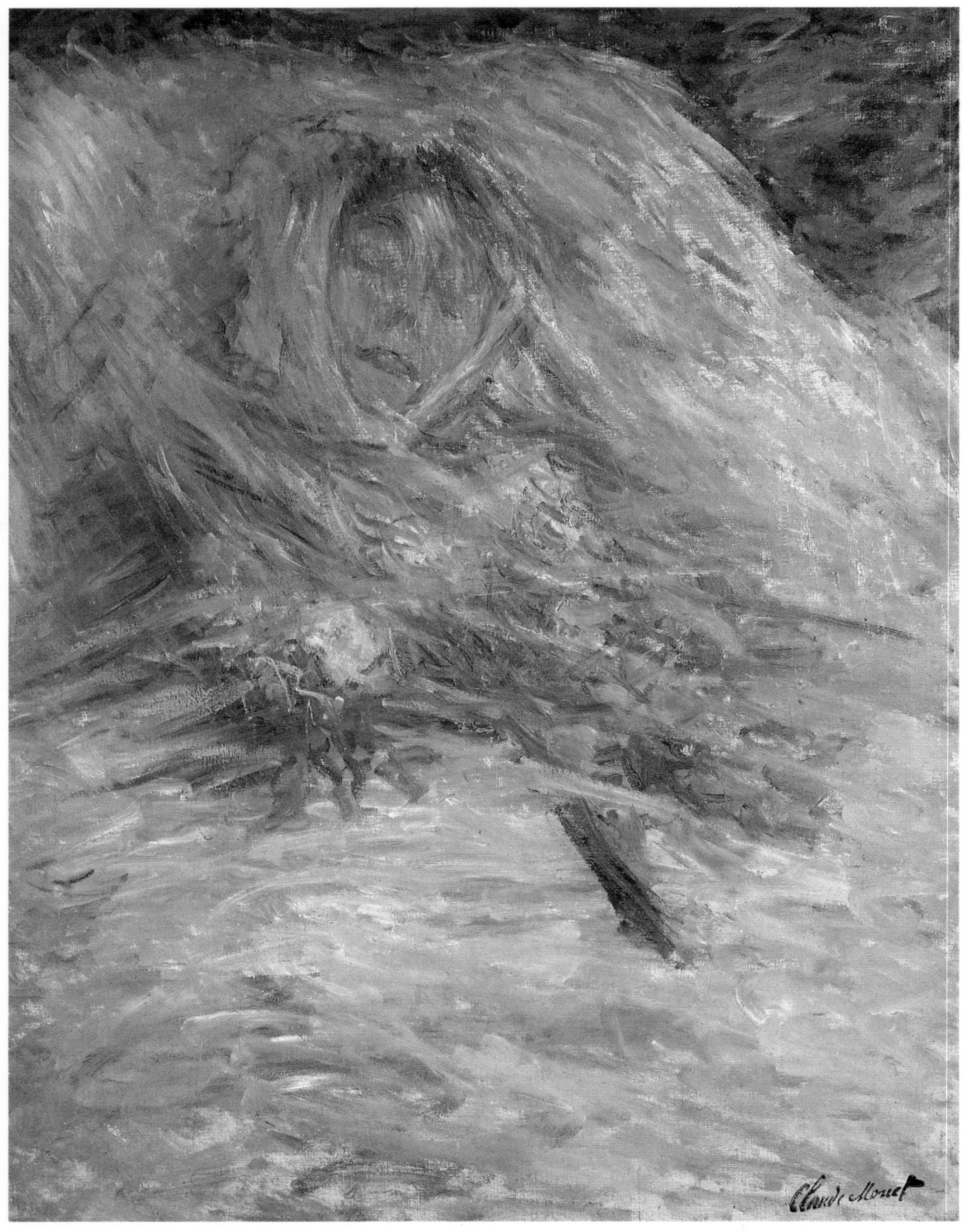

Camille Monet on her Deathbed, 1879
CLAUDE MONET, French, 1840–1926
Musée d'Orsay, Paris. Oil on canvas, 35 3/8 x 26 3/4 in.

Mourning and Loss

In art, as in life, the grief occasioned by the death of a lover may be expressed in different ways. The dramatic pose and the classical setting of Frederic, Lord Leighton's *Lachrymae* contrasts vividly with the poignantly understated naturalism of Claude Monet's *Camille on Her Death Bed*.

After the death of his first wife Camille, Monet described the benumbing effects of grief to a friend, revealing the depth of his commitment to naturalism: "One day, when I was at the deathbed of a woman who had been and still was very dear to me, I caught myself, my eyes fixed on her tragic forehead, in the act of mechanically analyzing the succession of appropriate color gradations which death was imposing on her immobile face. Tones of blue, of yellow, of gray, what have you? This is the point I had reached. Certainly it was natural to wish to record the last image of a woman who was departing forever. But even before I had the idea of setting down the features to which I was so deeply attached, my organism automatically reacted to the color stimuli, and my reflexes caught me up in spite of myself, in an unconscious operation which was the daily course of my life—just like an animal turning his mill." The contrast between the anguish implicit in the subject and the artist's extraordinarily objective approach creates a mood of muted pathos.

Lachrymae, by Frederic, Lord Leighton, is a good example of the enthusiasm that late-19th century academic painters felt for the glories of classical antiquity. In the picture, which draws its title from the Greek word for tears, a young woman stands grieving by the tomb of her lover. A wreath lies at the foot of the column, which has been adorned with diaphanous scarves, and the Greek vases and the flat cup suggest that offerings of oil have been made at the grave. A few dead leaves are scattered in the foreground, emphasizing the painting's mood of desolation.

Leighton based the figure of the young woman on a classical statue in the British Museum. In his work, he frequently combined a sculptural solidity of form with a strange and somewhat garish use of color. In the painting reproduced here, an unusual harmony of black, ivory, light green, and reddish-mauve is accentuated by the lurid orange of flames in the background. Like a number of 19th-century painters, Leighton turned away from the Iron Age of the Industrial Revolution to look back with nostalgia at the Golden Age of classical antiquity. Nonetheless, the sentimental pose of the young mourner and the black of her widow's weeds are closer in spirit to Victorian England than to Alexandrian Greece.

Lachrymae, c. 1895

FREDERIC, LORD LEIGHTON, British, 1830–1896

The Metropolitan Museum of Art, New York, Wolfe Fund, 1896, Catharine Lorillard Wolfe Collection. Oil on canvas, 62 x 24¾ in.

Enduring Fidelity

On this sarcophagus from an ancient Etruscan tomb, the terra cotta figures of a man and his wife recline together on a couch, as though participating at a festive banquet. In a moving gesture of affection, the man rests his wrist lightly on his wife's shoulder. Settled comfortably within his embrace, she raises her hands as if to emphasize a point in some serene, continuing conversation. The couple's youthful features have been modeled in the clay with a smooth economy of form. Their almond-shaped eyes and archaic smiles give them a vivacious and appealing expression.

This sarcophagus came from Cerveteri, a site near Rome that became a flourishing Etruscan settlement between the 8th and 4th centuries B.C. There a necropolis was built over the course of several centuries to contain tombs decorated in an evolving variety of styles. When these were excavated during the 19th century, archaeologists discovered wall paintings, fine Greek pottery, and native tomb sculpture such as the outstanding piece illustrated here. The cult of the dead was clearly an important part of Etruscan life, and sculptures such as this one were among the first images in human history to represent the dead as fully alive and enjoying themselves. In a work that is at once monumental and moving, sprightly and serene, the anonymous sculptor and his patrons have offered the viewer a touching view of love as the most enduring of life's pleasures.

Sarcophagus, from Cerveteri, c. 520 B.C.

ETRUSCAN

Museo Nazionale di Villa Giulia, Rome. Terracotta, length 79 in.

Come live with me and be my love,
And we will all the pleasures prove
That valleys, groves, hills and fields,
Woods, or steepy mountain yields.

And we will sit upon the rocks,
Seeing the shepherds feed their flocks,
By shallow rivers, to whose falls
Melodious birds sing madrigals.

And I will make thee beds of roses
And a thousand fragrant posies,
A cap of flowers, and a kirtle
Embroidered all with leaves of myrtle;

A gown made of the finest wool
Which from our pretty lambs we pull;
Fair lined slippers for the cold,
With buckles of the purest gold;

A belt of straw and ivy buds,
With coral clasps and amber studs:
And if these pleasures may thee move,
Come live with me, and be my love.

The shepherd swains shall dance and sing
For thy delight each May morning:
If these delights thy mind may move,
Then live with me and be my love.

CHRISTOPHER MARLOWE
The Passionate Shepherd to His Love

POSTSCRIPT

The Garden of Love

The Garden of Love

The image of an enchanted garden of love has appealed to artists since the Middle Ages, and works of art as diverse as medieval tapestries and rococo paintings (pages 58,59) portray pairs of elegant lovers in blossoming spring gardens.

Peter Paul Rubens' *Garden of Love* was painted shortly after the widowed artist married for the second time. His bride was the 16-year-old Hélène Fourment, and the artist's sense of wonder and renewal at the time of his marriage is clearly evident in the many portraits that he painted of her and of their children. In the work illustrated here, Rubens and his bride are visible at the left of the painting in an embrace that suggests that they are dancing. A cupid urges Hélène forward, as her husband stares at her lovely profile with a look of awe.

Around them, other couples converse and embrace, attended by a flying cloud of little cupids who scatter flowers on the lovers. In a fantastic baroque portico, a classical statue of the three graces can be seen, and at the picture's right edge, a fountain in the form of an ample woman astride a dolphin emphasizes the painting's mood of exuberant natural abundance.

Although at first glance, Wassily Kandinsky's *Improvisation Number 27: The Garden of Love* looks quite different from Rubens' painting, the two pictures both convey a mood of romantic, spontaneous pleasure by means of their freely painted forms. A large ocher-colored sun shines in the center of Kandinsky's landscape. Above it, a green couple lies embracing, and a second black and white couple recline in the foreground. A third pair of smaller gray figures can be seen at the left, sitting with their arms wrapped around one another. Black lines accentuate and anchor the floating areas of transparent color. One describes a bumpy ridge of ground in the lower left-hand corner of the painting, and others depict an undulating snake that enters the scene at the right, in front of a fence. A dog and a horse may also be represented in the painting. At the upper right, a waving form with gray lines across it indicates rain.

Kandinsky was one of the first artists to venture into experimentation with abstract art, beginning in 1910. An intensely theoretical artist, he hoped to develop a new pictorial language that could convey spiritual and emotional content without reliance on the details of external appearances. His choice of the Garden of Love as subject matter for this painting demonstrates the enduring fascination exerted by the image of a lovers' earthly paradise.

The Garden of Love, c. 1632–1634
PETER PAUL RUBENS, Flemish, 1577–1640
The Prado, Madrid. Oil on canvas, 78 x 111½ in.

Improvisation Number 27: The Garden of Love, 1912

WASSILY KANDINSKY, Russian, 1866–1944

The Metropolitan Museum of Art, New York, The Alfred Stieglitz Collection, 1949. Oil on canvas, 47 3/8 x 55 1/4 in.

FOLLOWING PAGES: DETAIL
The Garden of Love
PETER PAUL RUBENS

❧ A Lovers' Paradise

The two paintings illustrated here represent one of the most lasting and deeply rooted themes in Western art: the nostalgic dream of an arcadian world in which love is accepted spontaneously and openly as a natural element in a peaceful, rural landscape. The longing for a simple life spent in harmony with nature seems to be a natural outgrowth of life in sophisticated urban cultures. The image of an arcadian landscape originated in the writing of classical Roman poets such as Virgil, and its first appearance in art occurred in 16th-century Venice.

Concert Champêtre by Giorgione and/or Titian (pages 168–169) is the first great painting to express this pastoral dream, and it is the source of arcadian imagery that has persisted for nearly five centuries. Seated in the shade of a tree, a fashionably dressed young gentleman plays a lute as he leans toward an unkempt young rustic. A woman seated with them holds a flute, and a second pours a pitcher of water into a well. The women are lightly draped in an antique fashion. Nudity is their natural state, for as nymphs or local divinities, they personify this harmonious and enchanted landscape. In the distance at the right, a shepherd leads his flock. The man and his charges are also part of this classically inspired environment devoted to music, poetry, and love.

A distant descendant of the *Concert Champêtre* is Henri Rousseau's delightful painting *Happy Quartet*, which unites its arcadian imagery to another, equally rich pictorial tradition of a lovers' paradise: Adam and Eve in the Garden of Eden. The man's flute and the cupid attending the couple refer to the association of music and love, a central theme of arcadian imagery. However, the standing poses of the pair, and the modesty of the man's loincloth and the woman's strategically placed garland evoke traditional representations of Adam and Eve. As in the *The Marriage of Giovanni Arnolfini* by Jan van Eyck (page 106) the dog accompanying the couple is a symbol of fidelity.

A self-taught painter, Rousseau portrayed this happy scene with a directness and simplicity reminiscent of folk art. The painting has a naive and appealing charm that resonates with references to the enduring dream of a paradise where lovers live in enchanted harmony with nature and with one another.

Happy Quartet, c. 1902

HENRI ROUSSEAU (CALLED "LE DOUANIER"), French, 1844–1910

Mrs. John Hay Whitney. Oil on canvas, 37 x 22½ in.

FOLLOWING PAGES

Concert Champêtre (The Pastoral Concert), c. 1510

GIORGIO DA CASTELFRANCO, CALLED GIORGIONE, Italian, c. 1477–1510 AND/OR TIZIANO VECELLIO, CALLED TITIAN, Italian, c. 1487–1576

Musée du Louvre, Paris. Oil on canvas, 41¼ x 54 in.

About the Artists

Pierre Bonnard, French, 1867–1947 Pierre Bonnard began to paint while studying law in Paris. Inspired by the work of Paul Gaugin, he and a group of friends formed the artistic movement known as the Nabis, after the Hebrew word for prophet. During the 1890s, he was active as a lithographer and a theater designer, but after 1900, he devoted himself primarily to painting. Focusing on nudes, still lifes, landscapes, and intimate interiors, Bonnard never ceased to experiment with unusual compositions and with luminous, brilliant colors.

Sandro Botticelli, Italian, ca. 1445–1510 Alessandro Filipepi, known as Botticelli, was born in Florence during the period of the city's greatest artistic activity. He became a part of the circle of intellectuals around Lorenzo de Medici who were attempting to reconcile classical art and literature with Christianity. Botticelli was called to Rome by Pope Sixtus IV to paint frescos in the Sistine Chapel. At the end of his life, he was converted by the radical monk Savonarola and renounced his earlier, classically inspired work.

Constantin Brancusi, Romanian, 1876–1957 Constantin Brancusi was born to a family of peasant farmers in a remote area of Romania. Leaving home at the age of 11, he trained as a carpenter and stonemason. In 1904, after studying sculpture in Bucharest, he moved to Paris, where he met Auguste Rodin. Like other artists in Paris, Brancusi was attracted to the abstract forms of African sculpture, but he retained a lifelong interest in the woodcarving traditions of his homeland. Brancusi's dramatically simplified sculptural forms, carved from wood and stone or cast in polished bronze, exerted a tremendous influence on 20th-century sculpture.

CHAGALL: *The Bride and Groom of the Eiffel Tower*

Marc Chagall, Russian, 1887–1985 Born in Vitebsk, Marc Chagall studied in St. Petersburg, and lived in Paris from 1910 to 1914, where he was influenced by Cubism. After his return to Russia, he attempted to combine cubist style with imagery reflecting his Jewish heritage. In 1922, he left the Soviet Union, living first in Berlin and then in Paris, where he spent most of his long and successful career.

Gustave Courbet, French, 1819–1877 Jean-Désiré-Gustave Courbet was born in Ornans. After studying in Besançon and Paris, he came to prominence in 1850, when his large painting *Burial at Ornans* was attacked by critics. Courbet's flamboyance and his republican political views created controversy, but his interest in representing contemporary reality laid the foundation for the work of the Impressionists. Sentenced to heavy fines and a prison term for his participation in the Paris Commune of 1870, he spent the last years of his life in exile in Switzerland.

Francis Danby, Irish, 1793–1861 After studying in Dublin, Francis Danby visited London in 1813 and subsequently settled in Bristol, where he married and joined an informal society of artists. His early work consisted of small, naturalistic, intimate landscape paintings. Later, under the influence of J. M. W. Turner, he was drawn to more romantic and dramatic scenes. The scandal that arose when he eloped to Geneva with a mistress prevented his election to membership in the Royal Academy.

Joseph H. Davis, American, active 1830s Joseph Davis, who lived in Dover, New Hampshire, was one of the many self-taught American painters who flourished as professional portraitists during the second quarter of the 19th century. Working during the 1830s, Davis developed a style of watercolor portraiture notable for strong patterns and symmetrically placed figures.

Edgar Degas, French, 1834–1917 Hilaire Germain Edgar Degas was born in Paris, the son of a wealthy banker and his Creole wife. During his long career, he explored a wide range of contemporary urban subjects, creating sophisticated compositions observed from surprising points of view. A tireless experimenter in various media, he worked in oil paint, pastels, monoprints, photography, and sculpture. Although he exhibited with the Impressionists, his work was less concerned with effects of outdoor light than with the search for images that distilled revealing and typical gestures from fleeting moments of everyday reality.

Sir Anthony Van Dyck, Flemish, 1599–1641 Anthony Van Dyck was born in Antwerp, where he trained as a painter and served as the chief assistant to Peter Paul Rubens. After a visit to England and a prolonged stay in Italy, Van Dyck returned to Antwerp, where he completed a number of religious paintings. In 1631, he went to London, where he became the court painter to King Charles I and was knighted. Van Dyck developed a refined and elegant style of aristocratic court portraiture that set a pattern for two centuries of portrait painters, particularly in Britain.

Jan van Eyck, Netherlandish, ca. 1390–1441 Jan van Eyck worked for John of Bavaria, Count of Holland, and entered the service of Duke Philip the Good of Burgundy at Lille in 1424. In 1430, he moved to Bruges, where he enjoyed success as an artist and a diplomat. In 1432, he completed the great *Altarpiece of the Lamb* begun by his older brother Hubert, who died in 1426. Jan van Eyck's extraordinary ability to use the relatively new medium of oil paint to render light, atmosphere, space, and texture made him the greatest master of early Netherlandish painting.

Anselm Feuerbach, German, 1829–1880 Many of Anselm Feuerbach's works represent classical subject matter rendered in a carefully finished style that was influenced by the Parisian academic painter Thomas Couture. Feuerbach spent many years in Italy, and painted subjects from Italian literature as well as from classical mythology.

Jean-Honoré Fragonard, French, 1732–1806 Jean-Honoré Fragonard was born at Grasse, in the south of France, and studied with Jean-Baptiste-Siméon Chardin and François Boucher before traveling to Italy. Fragonard became a painter of intimate and lighthearted amorous scenes that afforded scope for his painterly brilliance. His broad and spontaneous style is also evident in many fine drawings in red chalk or brown ink wash.

VAN GOGH: *Public Garden with Couple and Blue Fir Tree*

Caspar David Friedrich, German, 1774–1840 Caspar David Friedrich studied in Copenhagen before settling in Dresden. The most important landscape painter of the German Romantic movement, he specialized in scenes portraying tiny human figures dwarfed by the vastness and power of nature. His paintings are characterized by unusual effects of light and by a meticulous finish that disguises the intervention of the artist's hand.

Thomas Gainsborough, British, 1727–1788 Thomas Gainsborough was born in Sudbury, in Suffolk, and trained in London, where he worked for an engraver. He returned to Sudbury around 1750, and in 1759, he moved to Bath, where he was discovered by the fashionable world. In 1774, he returned to London, where his reputation had preceded him. There his success continued, earning him the distinction—along with his rival Joshua Reynolds—of being the foremost portrait painter in England.

Paul Gauguin, French, (1848-1903) Paul Gauguin was born in Paris, but spent his early childhood in his mother's native Peru. He began to paint seriously in 1883. Leaving his family, he traveled to Brittany, where he developed a simplified style of painting which conveyed emotions through intensified color. Gauguin left France for Tahiti in 1891. His experimentation with ceramics and woodcuts extended the possibilities of those media, and his daring and brilliance as a colorist exerted a profound influence on later artists.

Giorgione, Italian, ca. 1477–1510 Giorgio da Castelfranco, known as Giorgione, studied with the Venetian painter Giovanni Bellini. Today he is best remembered for his development of a genre of pictures called *poesie*, small, brilliantly painted pictures that convey a poetic and evocative mood. Giorgione was a decisive influence on Titian's development, and during his short career, he significantly shaped the course of 16th-century Venetian painting.

Vincent van Gogh, Dutch, 1853–1890 The son of a minister, Vincent van Gogh worked as an art dealer, a teacher, and a missionary before beginning to paint in 1880. He lived for two years in Paris, where he was influenced by Impressionism. In 1888, he moved to Arles, in the South of France, where he developed a personal style of distinctive brushstrokes and intense colors. Van Gogh suffered his first attack of madness in December, 1888, and spent a year painting at an asylum in Saint-Rémy before moving to Auvers, where he worked until his suicide in July, 1890.

Dirck Hals, Dutch, 1591–1656 Dirck Hals was the younger brother of the better-known portraitist and genre painter Frans Hals. His work was similar in style to his brother's and included many lively genre scenes.

Suzuki Harunobu, Japanese, ca. 1725–1770 Suzuki Harunobu was a pioneer of the polychrome Japanese woodblock print, which developed around 1765. Producing over a thousand of these rich "brocade prints" before his death six years later, he contributed greatly to the technical development of the medium through his sophisticated color sense and use of embossing techniques. His delicate renditions of idealized girlhood achieved a grace and beauty unsurpassed by later artists.

Nicholas Hilliard, British, ca. 1547–1619 The son of an Exeter goldsmith, Nicholas Hilliard was associated with the court of Queen Elizabeth I, where he was licensed as a goldsmith, and painted fine miniature portraits of a kind used as keepsakes and sometimes worn as jewelry. Hilliard visited France in 1577/78, and the grace and elongated proportions of his figures in works such as the *Young Man Among Roses* (reproduced in this volume) evoke the elegant artistic style of the French court at Fontainebleau.

William Hogarth, British, 1697-1764 Born in London, William Hogarth trained as a silversmith and engraver. In 1730, he began to work on the narrative groups of paintings whose biting social satire brought him fame. Engravings after these series, which included *The Rake's Progress* and *Marriage à la Mode,* were so popular that Hogarth pressed for the introduction of a copyright law that would protect him from imitators.

Winslow Homer, American, 1836–1910 Born in Boston, Winslow Homer worked as a lithographer before studying art in New York. He covered the Civil War as an engraver for Harper's magazine, and painted scenes of American farm life. On a visit to Tynemouth, England, in the early 1880s, he turned to marine subjects, and after his move to Maine in 1883, he painted monumental scenes of the sea. Homer was a gifted watercolorist and produced many works in that medium on his travels.

Edward Hopper, American, 1882–1967 Born in Nyack, New York, Edward Hopper studied with Robert Henri, exhibited in the famous Armory show of 1913, and spent time in Paris before settling permanently in New York City. Turning away from European styles of abstraction, he developed a personal style notable for its strong, simple compositions and spare, light-filled interiors. Hopper's figures convey a sense of isolation that underscores the contemporary spirit of his work.

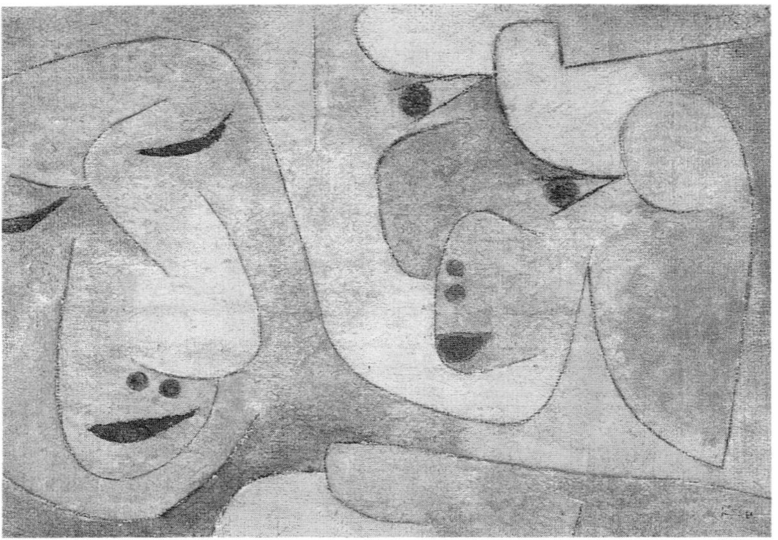

KLEE: *Old Married Couple*

Fra Filippo Lippi, Italian, ca. 1406–1469 An orphan, Fra Filippo Lippi entered a religious order in childhood. At the start of his artistic career he was greatly influenced by the monumental style of the Florentine painter Masaccio. Later he developed a more graceful and decorative approach, which significantly influenced Sandro Botticelli. While executing a painting commission at Prato, Fra Filippo met the nun Lucrezia Buti, with whom he eloped. Their son, Filippino Lippi, became a painter after studying with Botticelli.

Edouard Manet, French, 1832–1883 The early works of Parisian-born Edouard Manet reflected the artist's admiration for Diego Velásquez and Francisco Goya, as well as his determination to represent modern life. The scandals provoked in the 1860s by the exhibition of his *Déjeuner sur l'Herbe* and *Olympia* earned him a place among the leaders of the avant-garde, although the official recognition that he desired eluded him until the end of his life. Manet's integrity, directness, and fluid painterly style influenced the Impressionists, and in turn, Manet adopted the lighter palette of Impressionism during the last decade of his life.

Jean-Auguste-Dominique Ingres, French, 1780–1867 Born in Montauban, J. A. D. Ingres studied with Jacques-Louis David. A winner of the prestigious Prix de Rome, he traveled to Italy, where he remained for 18 years. After establishing a studio in Paris and gaining a reputation as a superb portrait painter, Ingres went back to Rome in 1834 to become the head of the French Academy there. He returned to Paris in 1841, where he enjoyed a long, successful career, remaining active until his death at the age of 87.

Wassily Kandinsky, Russian, 1866–1944 Wassily Kandinsky was born in Moscow, where he was trained as a lawyer. He began to paint at the age of 30, studying in Munich, and living for a year in Paris. Returning to Germany, he became a pioneer of abstract art, painting his first abstract work in 1910. He exhibited with the Russian avant-garde, was a founder of the German art movement *Der Blaue Reiter*, and taught at the Bauhaus. In 1933, he moved to Paris.

Paul Klee, Swiss, 1879–1940 Paul Klee was born in near Berne and studied in Munich, where he settled in 1906. There he met the artists of *Der Blaue Reiter*, an avant-garde group with whom he exhibited in 1912. His many small works in oils, watercolors, and graphic media are distinguished by a subtle wit, a sophisticated use of color, and his strong skill as a draftsman. Klee taught at the Bauhaus and was influential as a writer and art theorist.

Gustav Klimt, Austrian, 1862–1918 Gustav Klimt played an important role in the Vienna Secession movement, which was started by a group of Austrian artists who withdrew from the city's established academic art organizations in order to pursue modernist styles such as Art Nouveau. Richly ornamented with gold and patterns, Klimt's paintings include portraits and symbolic scenes. He completed a number of architectural murals, and his work was influential on Austrian decorative arts.

Isoda Koryusai, Japanese, active mid-1760s–1780s Beginning his career as a samurai, Isoda Koryusai later moved to Tokyo, where he became an *ukiyo-e* artist. Strongly influenced by the style of his friend and teacher Suzuki Harunobu, he signed his first works with the derivative name of Haruhiro. Koryusai became a specialist in the narrow, vertical "pillar prints" designed for display on the supporting columns of Japanese houses, and he produced a great number of erotic prints.

Frederic, Lord Leighton, British, 1830–1896 Born in Scarborough and brought up on the Continent, Frederic, Lord Leighton of Stretton studied art in Italy, Germany, France, and Belgium before moving to London in 1860. Initially achieving recognition as a painter of medieval subjects, he later turned to the classical themes for which he is best remembered today. He became president of the Royal Academy in 1878 and was raised to the peerage shortly before his death.

Roy Lichtenstein, American, 1923– Born in New York City, Roy Lichtenstein studied at the Art Students League, and at Ohio State University, where he also taught. Returning to New York City in 1963, he became an important contributor to the movement known as Pop Art, producing paintings, prints, and sculpture that incorporated references to a wide range of commercial and artistic styles. He moved to outhampton, New York, in 1970, and continues to exhibit widely.

Henri Matisse, French, 1869–1954 After training as a lawyer, Henri Matisse began to paint around 1890. By 1905, he was acknowledged as the leader of an artistic group known as the Fauves, or "wild beasts" because of their use of intense color. A daring draftsman and a brilliant colorist, Matisse painted a series of monumental, simplified canvases before moving to Nice in 1917. There, he turned to intimate interiors. At the end of his life, he produced large collages of cut and painted paper that further extended his enormous influence on 20th-century art.

Claude Monet, French, 1840-1926 Claude Monet was raised in Le Havre, where he was encouraged to paint outdoors by the older artist Eugène Boudin. After studying in Paris, where he met Camille Pissarro, Paul Cézanne, Auguste Renoir, and Alfred Sisley, Monet began to render landscapes in terms of light and atmosphere. The loosely painted, sketchlike appearance of his 1872 canvas, *Impression Sunrise* gave rise to the derisive term "Impressionists," coined by a critic to describe the group of artists who exhibited together between 1874 and 1886. after early years of poverty, Monet finally attained recognition and financial success in 1889. He bought the house at Giverny where he had lived since 1883 and created a Japanese garden that became the inspiration for his waterlily paintings.

Hishikawa Kichibei Moronobu, Japanese, ca. 1625–1694 Born across the bay from Tokyo, Hishikawa Moronobu studied painting while working in his family's dyeing and embroidery business. He evidently moved to Tokyo in the 1660s, where he became the first major artist of *ukiyo-e* printmaking after black and white woodblock prints were published from his drawings. Moronobu was also a prolific book illustrator and a painter. His strong graphic style shaped the course of Japanese woodblock printing for two centuries.

William Sidney Mount, American, 1807–1868 Born on rural Long Island, William Sidney Mount apprenticed in his brother's sign-painting shop and studied in New York, where he gained a reputation as a painter of portraits and genre scenes. Returning to live on Long Island, he developed a clear and luminous style. His scenes of rural life appealed to the nostalgia of city dwellers who were raised in the country, and engravings after his paintings enjoyed great popularity.

William Mulready, Irish, 1786–1863 William Mulready was born in County Clare but grew up in London. He studied at the Royal Academy, where he later taught the young artists who eventually formed the Pre-Raphaelite group. Supporting his early work as a landscape artist by painting theater scenery, he gradually achieved success with his small-scale, brightly-colored genre scenes.

Edvard Munch, Norwegian, 1863–1944 Edvard Munch studied in Oslo and lived in Paris from 1889–1892, where he encountered the Symbolist movement and learned from the work of Vincent van Gogh and Paul Gauguin. Munch's paintings and prints received wide exposure in Paris and Berlin around the turn of the century, where they impressed numerous artists, including Pierre Bonnard and the German Expressionists.

Charles Willson Peale, American, 1741–1827 Trained as a craftsman, Charles Willson Peale studied in London with the American artist Benjamin West. Settling in Philadelphia, he encouraged the artistic careers of his brother, his nieces, and his sons Rembrandt, Raphaelle, Rubens, and Titian. He also founded the first American art school, and established the country's first museum, which contained the reassembled skeleton of a mastodon that the artist had unearthed in 1801.

Peithinos, Greek, active 5th century B.C. Peithinos was one of the many gifted artists of the early red-figure style of Greek vase-painting, in which backgrounds were painted with an iron-rich clay that turned black when fired and the figures retained the red color of the pottery. This style, which gradually supplanted the earlier black-figure painting, developed in Athens during the early years of its democracy.

Pablo Picasso, Spanish, 1881-1973 The son of an artist, Pablo Picasso studied in Barcelona before moving to Paris in 1904. His work became strongly experimental around 1906, and from 1907 to 1914 he worked closely with the French artist Georges Braque to develop Cubism, a new style of painting that became one of the most influential artistic styles of the 20th century. A prolific artist and a tireless experimenter, Picasso worked in painting, collage, printmaking, sculpture, ceramics, and theater design.

REZA-YE ' ABBASI: *Courtly Lovers*

Pinturicchio, Italian, ca. 1454–1513 Bernardino di Betto, called Pinturicchio, was a follower of the Umbrian artist Perugino, whom he assisted when the older master was called to Rome by Pope Sixtus IV to paint frescoes in the Sistine Chapel. Later Pinturicchio returned to Rome to carry out a painting commission for Pope Alexander VI. Pinturicchio's attractive and colorful works offer an appealing picture of courtly life in Renaissance Italy.

Nicolas Poussin, French, 1594–1665 Born in Normandy, Nicolas Poussin lived in Paris before traveling to Rome in 1624, where he was greatly influenced by the Eternal City's ancient ruins, and by the paintings of Raphael and Titian. In 1640, he was called back to Paris by King Louis XIII to head the French Academy, but he returned to Rome 18 months later. He remained in Rome for the rest of his life, producing landscape studies of great freshness and classical compositions that became the basis for more than two centuries of French academic painting. His works have influenced painters from Jacques-Louis David to Paul Cézanne.

Francesco Primaticcio, Italian, 1504–1570 Francesco Primaticcio was one of the late Renaissance artists who painted in a style known as Mannerism. This experimental style was characterized by elongated figures, exaggerated poses, and unusual compositions and color schemes. He was invited by the French King Francis I to Fontainebleau, where he decorated the Gallery of Ulysses. Primaticcio worked as a sculptor and architect, but few traces of his large decorative projects survive.

Rembrandt Harmensz. van Rijn, Dutch, 1606-1669 Rembrandt studied in Leiden and Haarlem before settling in Amsterdam in 1631. He married Saskia van Uylenburgh in 1634, and experienced a period of great productivity and success. After Saskia's death in 1642, his financial position deteriorated sharply but in spite of his poverty, he remained a prolific and influential artist, producing paintings, drawings, and etchings notable for their rich effects of light and shadow and for the artist's sympathetic understanding of the human condition.

Pierre Auguste Renoir, French, 1841–1919 Born in Limoges, Pierre Auguste Renoir moved to Paris in 1845. There he worked as a porcelain painter before studying at the Ecole des Beaux-Arts, where he met Claude Monet.

TITIAN: *Venus and Adonis*

Between 1867 and 1870, Renoir and Monet painted outdoors together, developing a style of broken brushwork to express the changing light and atmosphere of the landscape. Renoir exhibited in four of the eight Impressionist exhibitions, but later turned to a more sculptural style of draftsmanship.

Reza-ye 'Abbasi, Iranian, active early 17th century Reza-ye Abbasi was a painter to the imperial court of the Persian Safavid dynasty at Isfahan during the early decades of the 17th century. When he became the favored painter to the Sultan Shah Abbas, he changed his name from Aqa Reza to Reza-ye Abbasi. Reza developed a style that was notable for its calligraphic line, subdued color and sensuous treatment of figures and draperies. This style was widely copied by later artists.

Theodore Robinson, American, 1852-1896 Born in Vermont, Theodore Robinson studied in Chicago, New York, and Paris. In 1884, after working in New York, he traveled to Europe, where he lived for eight years. During this time, he visited Claude Monet at Giverny. His canvases show the influence of the great French Impressionist, although the descriptive realism of their solidly drawn forms is characteristic of American painting.

Henri Rousseau, French, 1844–1910 The self-taught Henri Rousseau, sometimes called "Le Douanier," or Customs Inspector, after his profession, began to paint full time after his retirement from civil service in 1885. Around 1906, he met Pablo Picasso and other members of the Parisian avant-garde, who were enthusiastic about the imaginative power and naive directness of his work.

Peter Paul Rubens, Flemish, 1577–1640 After completing a classical education, Peter Paul Rubens traveled and worked for eight years in Italy before settling permanently in Antwerp, where he pursued a successful career as a court painter and diplomat. His admiration for Titian led him to develop a style of rich color and fluent brushwork that became one of the major influences on later European painting. After the death of his first wife, Isabella Brandt, in 1630, the artist married the 16-year old Hélène Fourment, who appeared frequently in his later paintings.

John Singer Sargent, American, 1856–1925 Born and raised in Florence, Italy, John Singer Sargent studied in Paris before settling in London, where he became a fashionable portrait artist known for the dazzling bravura of his paintings. An admirer of Diego Velásquez and a friend of the Impressionists, Sargent also painted informal and appealing genre scenes and watercolors.

Raphael Soyer, American, 1899–1987 Raphael Soyer was born in Russia and emigrated to America with his family in 1912. The Soyers lived in Philadelphia for a year before settling in New York City, where the artist studied at Cooper Union, the National Academy of Design, and the Art Students League. Soyer belonged to a group of figure painters who rejected European modernist styles such as Cubism in favor of realistic, sympathetic portrayals of New York's working class.

Jan Steen, Dutch, 1625/6–1679 The son of a brewer, Jan Steen attended the university at Leiden, where he spent most of his career. A prolific painter of great narrative and comic gifts, Steen specialized in moralizing genre scenes, often representing tavern interiors and convivial gatherings.

Gerard ter Borch, Dutch, 1617–1681 The son of a painter, Gerard ter Borch was born in Zwolle. He traveled widely in Europe before settling in Deventer, where he enjoyed a successful career. His early paintings represented barracks and guardroom scenes, but his later work consisted of elegant interiors in which small groups of figures converse or play music. Ter Borch's work is notable for the delicacy and grace of his female figures and for his ability to render the shimmering texture of satin.

Tintoretto, Italian, 1518-1594 The son of a dyer, Jacopo Robusti, known as Tintoretto, was an energetic and ambitious painter who ran a large workshop and executed many important commissions in Venice, including the vast painting cycle on the ceiling of the Scuola di San Rocco. He developed a style that was notable for dramatic effects of light and dynamic compositions.

Titian, Italian, ca. 1487–1576 Tiziano Vecellio, known as Titian, was born in mountainous Pieve di Cadore, near Venice, and studied with Giovanni Bellini. Influenced by his fellow-student Giorgione, he developed a rich painterly style that has exerted a profound influence on European painting since the Renaissance. During his long and sucessful career, he carried out numerous royal commissions, and produced altarpieces, mythological paintings, and portraits.

Tanjodo Ishikawa Shuha Toyonobu, Japanese, 1711–1785 An early artist of the Japanese woodblock print, Ishikawa Toyonobu followed in the footsteps of Okumura Masanobu. In turn, his handcolored prints of standing young women influenced the work of his younger contemporary, Suzuki Harunobu.

Kitagawa Utamaro, Japanese, 1753–1806 Beginning his career as a book illustrator, Kitagawa Utamaro rose to prominence as a printmaker during the period when the colored woodblock print reached the height of its popularity. Best known for his portrayal of female figures, from courtesans to tea-house beauties and working women, he produced a large body of erotic prints, and became the first Japanese printmaker whose work received widespread exposure in the West.

WATTEAU: *Mezzetin*

Jan Vermeer, Dutch, 1632–1675 Jan Vermeer was born in Delft and worked there as an artist and picture dealer. He became the president of the painters guild, but more than half of his known work was unsold in his studio at the time of his death at age 43. Vermeer worked with a camera obscura to construct his carefully composed images, which shimmer with a brilliantly-observed light.

Paolo Veronese, Italian, ca. 1528-1588 Known as Veronese, after his birthplace, Verona, Paolo Caliari was a successful and prolific painter, who executed numerous commissions for large canvases in a rich and opulent style similar to that of his older contemporary Titian. His work, notable for its refined and sophisticated color harmonies, was a major influence on later Venetian painters.

Edouard Vuillard, French, 1868–1940 Edouard Vuillard studied in Paris, where he met Pierre Bonnard, with whom he formed the group that called itself the Nabis, after the Hebrew word for prophet. Vuillard's early work is notable for its dense pattern, broken brushwork, and bright color. His later work was more conservative, and the reclusive artist rarely exhibited after 1914.

Jean Antoine Watteau, French, 1684–1721 Born in Valenciennes, Antoine Watteau traveled to Paris in 1702, where he encountered the work of Peter Paul Rubens. He was admitted to the Royal Academy as an associate member in 1712, and as a full member in 1717, when the special category of *fêtes galantes* was created to describe his poetic, pastoral landscapes peopled with lovers and theatrical characters. Notable for outstanding draftsmanship and delicate color, Watteau's paintings often convey a poignant sense of nostalgia.

Index of Artists and Illustrations

G. FUMAGALLI